Contents

Living processes

All plants and animals have five life processes which keep them alive.

Human beings are living things and although they are different from plants, they all do certain things – they grow, reproduce, move, need nutrients and are sensitive.

Here are the five life processes:

1 Grow – All living things grow bigger and bigger.

2 Reproduce – this means 'to make more'. New plants grow from seeds. Animals have young.

3 Move – living things move. Leaves turn towards the light and roots grow down towards the soil. Animals move their bodies.

4 Need nutrients – living things need food to provide them with energy to move and grow. Most plants make their own food by using sunlight. Animals eat plants or other animals.

5 Sensitivity – living things are aware of how their surroundings change and respond to them.

This will help...

. . . you remember the five life processes:

Giraffes (grow)
Ride (reproduce)
My (movement)
New (nutrition)
Skateboard (sensitivity)!

Did you know?

Seeds are often still alive although they might look as if they are dead.

Try these

1 What does sensitivity mean?
2 Plants can move by themselves. True or false?

If you know your stuff...
grow
get bigger
reproduce
...you'll spot the odd one out.

Puzzle code

Which one is not a life process:

growth **(O)**, nutrition **(P)**, photosynthesis **(N)**, reproduction **(M)**?

Write the letter in the grid on page 64.

REMEMBER

Something is not alive unless it does all five life processes.

On your toes What is the sentence to help you remember the five life processes?

Human life cycle

Revise wise

Humans are born as babies and change as they grow older. Adult humans produce more babies. This is called the human life cycle.

This will help...

Think about the ways in which you have changed since you were a baby.
What can you do now that you couldn't do then?

Like all other plants and animals, humans are produced by reproduction. From a fertilised egg, a tiny baby grows inside its mother and is totally dependent on her for protection, oxygen and food. Once born, the baby grows as it get older. It becomes a child, a teenager and eventually an adult. Adult humans then produce new babies.

Did you know?

It takes about nine months for a baby to fully grow inside its mother's womb.

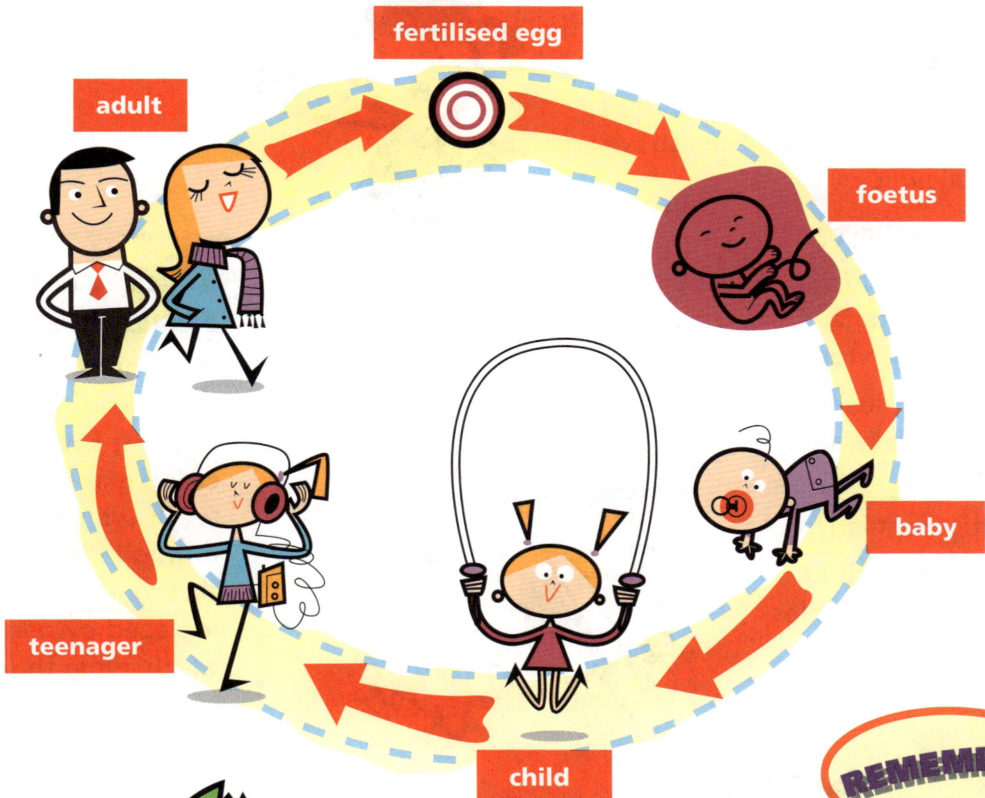

Try these

1 The stages that humans go through as they get older is called the human ________ ________ .

2 Humans stay exactly the same throughout their whole lives. True or false?

If you know your stuff...

teenager

singer

foetus

...you'll spot the odd one out.

REMEMBER

Humans change as they go through the different parts of the life cycle. When we are babies and children we need lots of help from our parents.

Puzzle code

The next stage in the human life cycle after childhood is:

teenager **(O)**, foetus **(P)**, adult **(Q)**.

Write the letter in the grid on page 64.

On your toes What is the name given to the process by which more animals or plants are created?

Teeth

Revise wise

Humans have three types of teeth: molars, canines and incisors, which crush, tear and cut food.

This will help...

Canine means 'to do with dogs'. Your canine teeth are your 'fangs', which are used for ripping meat!

All food has to be cut up and crushed into tiny pieces so we can swallow it.

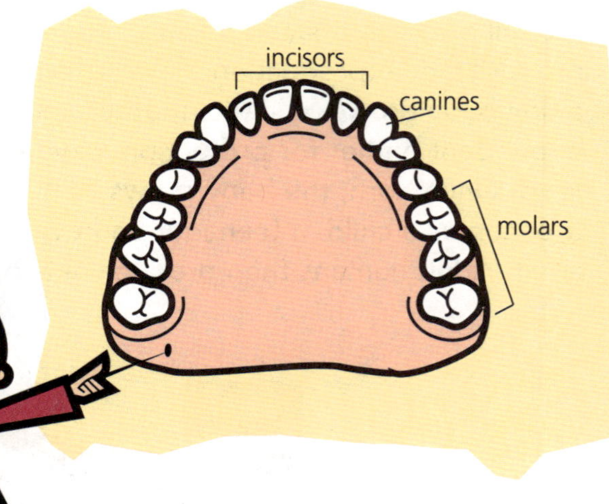

Different types of teeth

Look into a mirror to see three different types of teeth. Each one has a special job to do.

Incisors: front teeth for **cutting** food. You use them to bite into food.

Canines: pointed side teeth for **gripping and tearing** food. They are long and sharp.

Molars: back teeth for **crushing and grinding** food. They are used to break food down into very small pieces so we can swallow it.

Looking after your teeth

The food we eat can damage our teeth. Sugar left in the mouth is eaten by bacteria. This forms plaque, which rots away the enamel on the tooth and creates a hole.

1 Brush your teeth at least twice a day, especially after eating sweet food.
2 Visit the dentist regularly.
3 Eat healthy foods. such as crunchy fruit and vegetables, plenty of milk and not too many sweets!

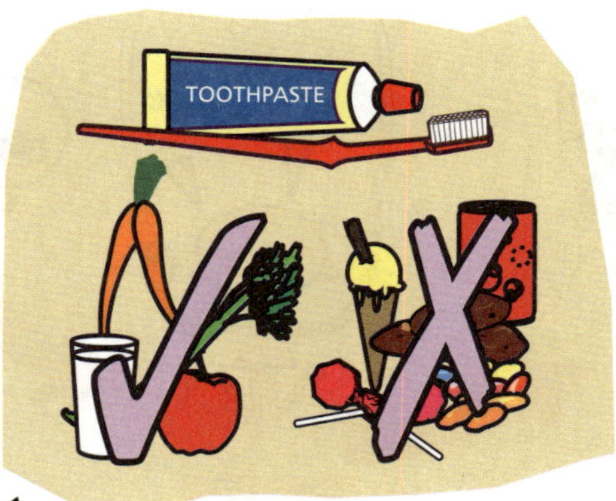

Did you know?

Humans have two sets of teeth. The first set is called milk teeth, which comes through from about six months old. These are replaced by permanent teeth, which come through from about five years old.

Try these

1 Sugar in foods is eaten by bacteria which creates ________ .

2 Teeth used for tearing meat are called incisors. True or false?

If you know your stuff...

incisors
canines
plaque
molars

...you'll spot the odd one out.

REMEMBER

Humans have three types of teeth to make sure the food is small enough to be swallowed.

Puzzle code

Molars are teeth used for:

cutting **(X)**, tearing and gripping **(V)**, crushing and grinding **(W)**.

Write the letter in the grid on page 64.

 On your toes What causes plaque?

Food

Revise wise

To keep healthy, grow and be active, humans need a varied and balanced diet.

Your body needs food to grow, repair itself, get energy for activities and to keep healthy. Different foods have different jobs to do, so it is important that we eat a **balanced diet**. If we eat too much of one type of food it can make us unhealthy.

Did you know?

70 % of our bodies are made up of water, so it is very important to drink lots of water.

Food groups

We can put food into different groups depending on what they do for our body.

For growth and repair, we need foods containing **proteins** – meat, fish eggs, milk, nuts.	
For energy, we need foods containing **carbohydrates** (bread, chips, pasta, rice) and fats (cakes, biscuits, butter, cheese).	
For healthy cells, we need foods containing **vitamins** and minerals – fruit, vegetables.	
For healthy intestines, we need food containing **fibre** – fruit, vegetables, brown bread, cereals.	

Too many of these could be bad for your health.

This will help...

Can **F**ree **F**ish **M**ake **V**eggie **P**ies?
Carbohydrates **F**ats **F**ibre **M**inerals **V**itamins **P**roteins

Try these

1 Fats give us energy. True or false?
2 A ________ is what we eat and drink.

Puzzle code

Which of these are very high in vitamins and minerals:

- pasta and cereals **(S)**
- fruit and vegetables **(T)**
- meat and fish **(U)**?

Write the letter in the grid on page 64.

If you know your stuff…

carbohydrates
vitamins
diet
proteins

…you'll spot the odd one out.

REMEMBER

It is important that we eat food from each of the different groups to have a varied and balanced diet.

If you eat too many energy foods without doing enough activity then the extra energy will be stored as fat.

On your toes Why is fibre important in your diet?

Body organs

Revise wise

Your body contains very important parts, called organs, which do special jobs.

This will help...

Think of the organs as different parts of a car engine, working together to make the car (your body) run. If one part stops working the engine won't work properly.

An organ is a part of the body with a special **function**. They keep the body working – without them we would die. Important organs are the heart, lungs, brain, kidneys, liver and a group of organs called the digestive system.

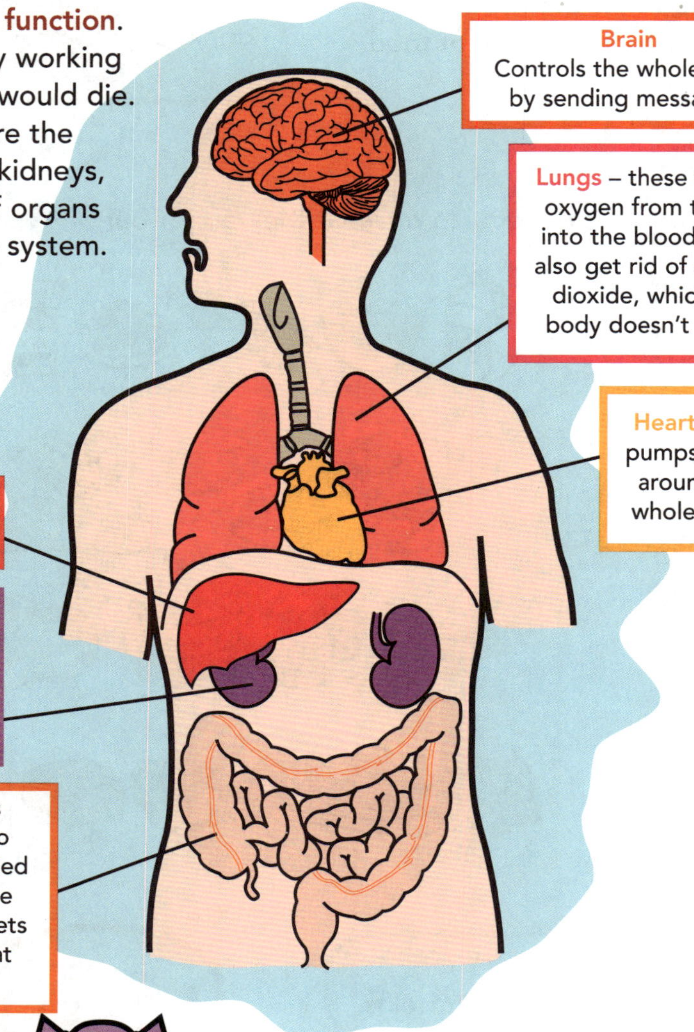

Brain
Controls the whole body by sending messages.

Lungs – these take in oxygen from the air into the blood. They also get rid of carbon dioxide, which the body doesn't need.

Heart – this pumps blood around the whole body.

Liver – this stores and controls chemicals.

Kidneys – these clean the blood by removing waste substances and make urine, which is stored in the bladder.

Digestive system – this breaks down the food so the goodness can be carried in the bloodstream to the rest of the body. It also gets rid of the substances that cannot be used.

Did you know?

Part of the digestive system is called the small intestine. This tube is about seven metres long. It is curled round and round so it all fits in the body.

Try these

1 What do the kidneys do?
2 The brain is the place where all the thoughts and feelings happen. True or false?

Puzzle code

The digestive system:

- breaks down food **(H)**
- is a control centre for the body **(J)**
- stores vitamins **(K)**.

Write the letter in the grid on page 64.

If you know your stuff…

brain
blood
lungs

…you'll spot the odd one out.

REMEMBER

Each organ has a special job to do and they all work together to keep you alive.

On your toes The kidneys, brain, heart and lungs are all ________.

The heart

The heart is the important organ that acts as a pump. It circulates blood around the body.

This will help...

Think about the word **circle** which means 'round'. **Circulation** is the way blood goes 'round' the body.

Your blood carries important substances, such as oxygen and digested food, around the body. The heart pumps the blood to the lungs where it collects oxygen, then it goes back to your heart. Then, the heart pumps the blood around the rest of the body. The body uses up the oxygen so the blood must be pumped back to the heart so it can collect more oxygen from the lungs. This is called **circulation of the blood**.

Did you know?

The vessels carrying the blood away from the heart are called **arteries**.

The vessels carrying the blood back to the heart are called **veins**. Many veins are near the surface of the skin – that's why we can see them.

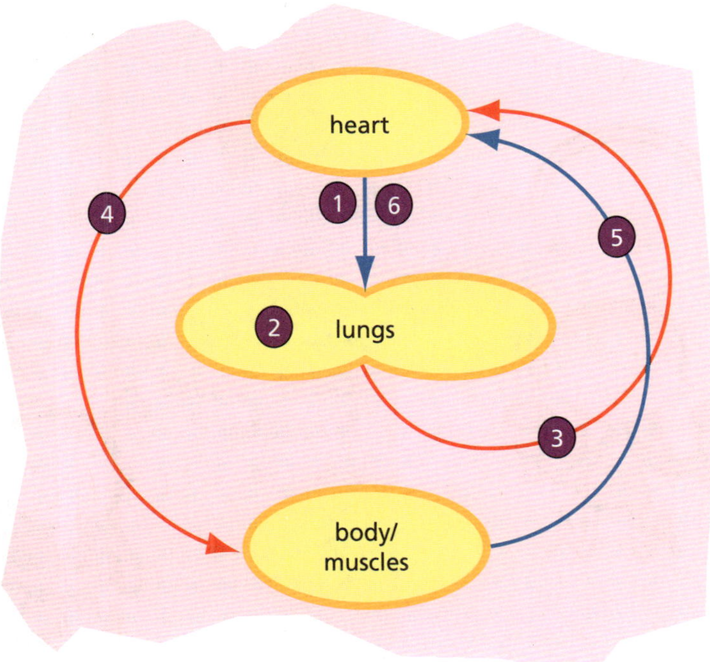

Here are the main stages of the circulation of the blood:

1 The heart pumps blood to the lungs.

2 The blood picks up oxygen in the lungs.

3 The blood, containing the oxygen, goes back to the heart.

4 The heart pumps the blood around the body to the muscles.

5 The muscles use up the oxygen, so the blood has to be pumped back to the heart in order to pick up oxygen in the lungs.

6 The whole cycle starts again.

Try these

1 After the blood has been pumped around the body it then goes to the lungs. True or false?

2 Blood is pumped by the ________ .

Puzzle code

After the blood has picked up oxygen in the lungs:

- it is circulated around the body **(E)**
- it returns to the heart **(A)**
- it goes to the lungs **(O)**.

Write the letter in the grid on page 64.

If you know your stuff…

artery

blood

vein

…you'll spot the odd one out.

REMEMBER

The heart pumps the blood to the lungs to collect oxygen before it travels around the rest of the body.

On your toes What part of the skeleton protects the heart and lungs?

Pulse rate

Revise wise

When you exercise, your pulse rate increases. This is because your heart beats faster.

When you do any exercise, your muscles need more energy to make them work harder. They get this energy from the **food** and **oxygen** carried by the blood. This means the heart has to beat faster to send more blood around the body to the muscles. That's why your pulse rate gets faster when you exercise.

This will help...

Think about what happens to your body when you exercise. Try feeling your pulse.

What is your pulse rate?

Every time your heart beats, there is a rush of blood along the arteries, away from the heart. You can feel a throb in your wrist or neck. This is what we call our **pulse**. Press lightly with one or two fingers on your wrist. Count how many times you can feel the pulse in a minute.

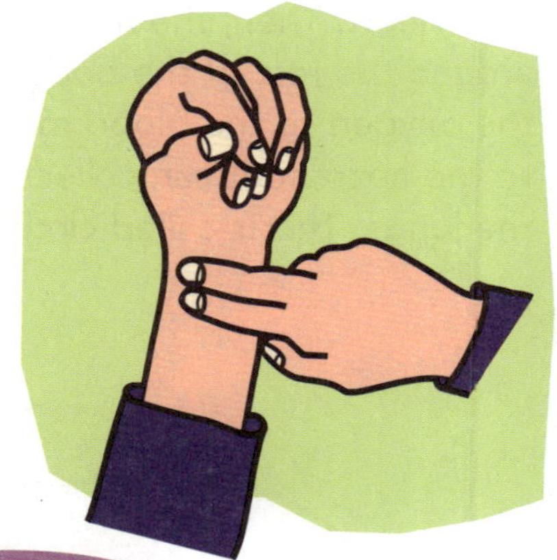

What happens when you exercise?

1. When you do any exercise your muscles need more energy to make them work harder.
2. The heart has to beat faster and you breathe faster so that more food and oxygen can be pumped to the muscles.
3. After you have stopped exercising your pulse rate will slowly return to normal.

Did you know?

When you are resting, your pulse rate is about 70 beats per minute.

Try these

1. Good places to feel your pulse are your ________ and ________ .
2. During exercise breathing slows down. True or false?

Puzzle code

The organ that supplies oxygen to the blood is:

the heart **(P)**, the liver **(S)**, the lungs **(T)**.

Write the letter in the grid on page 64.

If you know your stuff...

pulse rate

heart beat

water

...you'll spot the odd one out.

REMEMBER

Not only does your pulse rate increase when you do any exercise, you also have to breathe faster and your body gets hotter.

On your toes What do your muscles need when you exercise?

The skeleton

Bones inside the body are joined together. This is called the skeleton.

Human beings are supported by a framework of strong, hard bones inside the body called a skeleton. The skeleton does three things:

1 it protects the vital organs inside your body

2 it supports the body so that it can stand up

3 it enables the body to move.

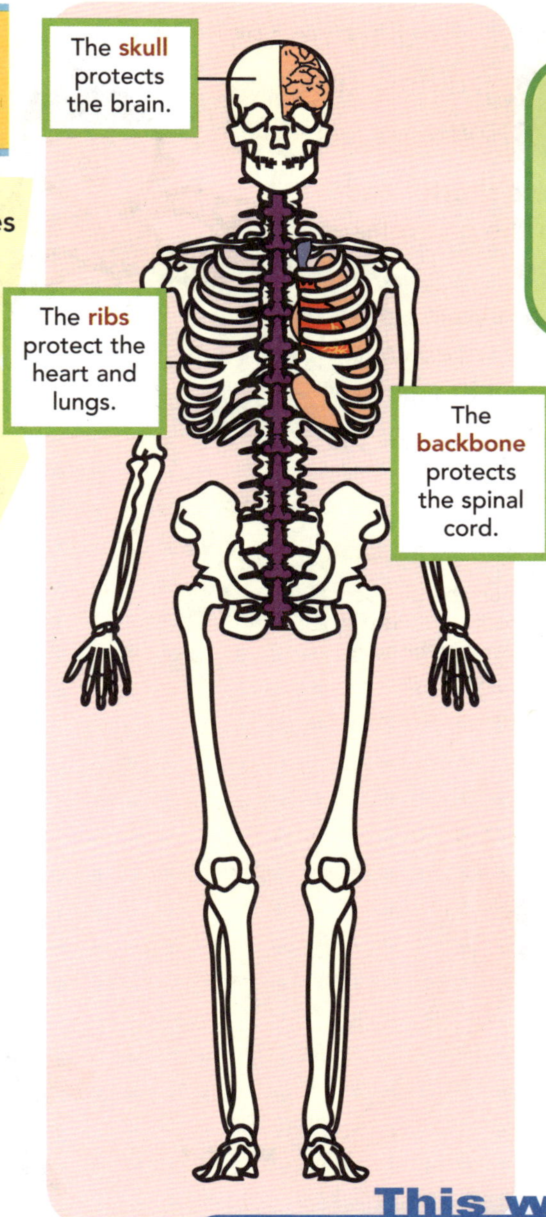

Protection

The skeleton protects the soft organs inside your body.

Support

Your skeleton helps you to stand upright and holds all the body parts in place.

Did you know?

The human skeleton is made up of 206 bones.

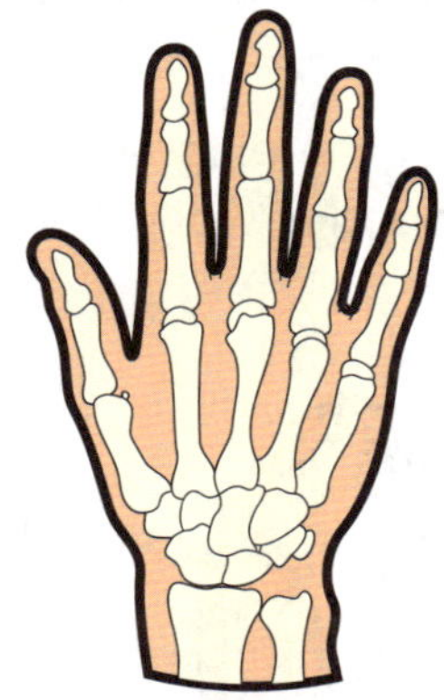

Movement

Many parts of the skeleton are jointed so that the body can bend, for example, arms, legs, fingers. Muscles are joined to the bones and work in pairs – see page 10 to find out more about muscles.

This will help...

Feel around your own body to find bones and joints.

Try these

1 The skull protects the heart. True or false?

2 The bone that protects the spinal cord is called the _______ .

Puzzle code

The ribs protect the:

- heart and lungs **(A)**
- the spinal cord **(B)**
- the brain **(C)**.

Write the letter in the grid on page 64.

If you know your stuff...

skull

ribs

brain

backbone

...you'll spot the odd one out.

REMEMBER

The three important functions of the skeleton are to protect, move and support the body.

Moving muscles

Pairs of muscles are attached to bones and they work in pairs, pulling the bones to make them move.

As one muscle **contracts** (gets shorter and thicker), the other muscle in the pair **relaxes** (becomes longer and thinner).

When you bend and straighten your arm, two muscles are working – the triceps and biceps. Move your arm and feel the muscles.

Look at the diagram (below) to see how the arm muscles work in a pair.

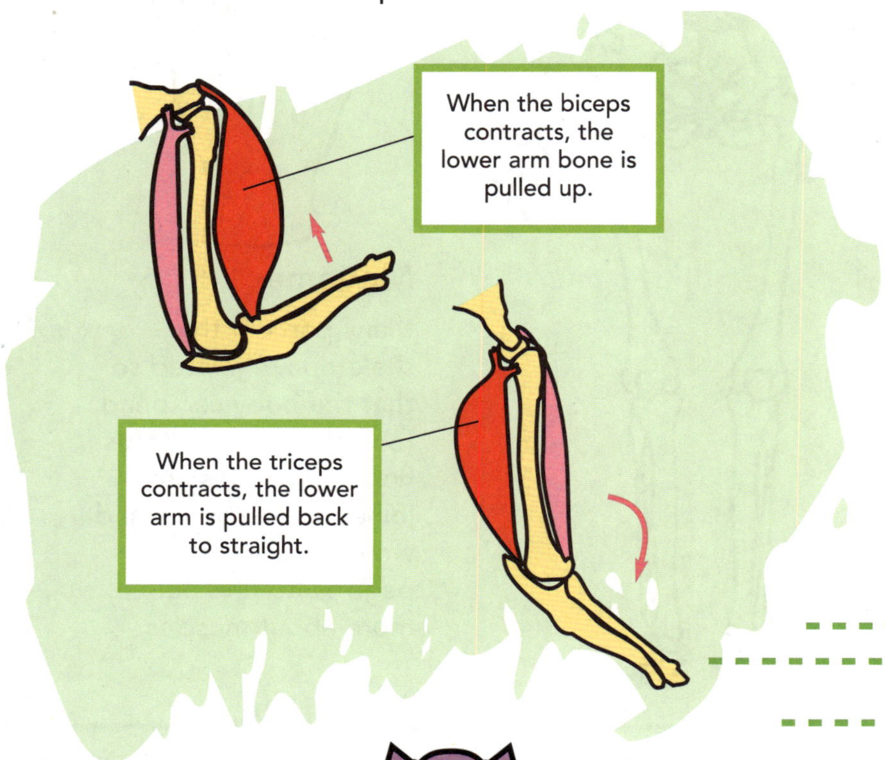

This will help...

Muscles are like squashy springs. They can get shorter and spring back but if you stretch them they can be damaged.

Did you know?

Your heart is mostly made from muscle. It moves without us thinking about it.

When we exercise, the muscles need to work harder. So the muscles need more oxygen and food to make energy. That is why the heart has to pump faster to get more blood to the muscles.

Try these

1 Contract means ___ ________ .
2 Muscles become thicker when they contract. True or false?

Puzzle code

When muscles are working in pairs to make us move:

- both muscles are relaxed **(M)**
- one muscle is relaxed and the other is contracted **(L)**
- both muscles are contracted **(N)**.

Write the letter in the grid on page 64.

If you know your stuff...

contract
lengthen
thicken
shorten

...you'll spot the odd one out.

REMEMBER

Muscles always work in pairs, one muscle relaxes (becomes longer) while the other contracts (gets shorter).

On your toes How many muscles work together so you can move part of your body?

Dangerous drugs

Revise wise

Some substances affect the way the body works. These are called drugs.

There are some substances, such as **alcohol**, **tobacco** and **drugs**, which can be very dangerous to your health. They affect different parts of your body. People who misuse drugs can become **addicted** to them, then they need to take the drugs every day and their bodies cannot do without them.

This will help...

Drugs, tobacco and alcohol all contain chemicals which affect the way your body works.

Did you know?

Smokers are three times more likely to have a heart attack than non-smokers.

Alcohol

In small amounts it is not harmful and it can make people feel relaxed.

Harmful effects: slows down reaction time, dangerous for driving.
Heavy drinking: damages the liver, heart, stomach and brain.

Tobacco
Contains a lot of tar. This collects in the lungs and affects breathing.

Harmful effects on the lungs: breathing problems and diseases. **Examples:** bronchitis and lung cancer.
Harmful effects on the heart: blocks the arteries and causes heart attacks.

Drugs

Doctors prescribe drugs as medicines, to make us better. They are only harmful if they are not used properly.

Harmful effects: they can cause damage to the brain.
Examples: heroin and cocaine.

Try these

1 Drugs given by doctors help us to get well. These drugs are m _ _ _ _ _ _ _ _ _.

2 All drugs can be dangerous if they are not used properly. True or false?

Puzzle code

Drugs, alcohol and tobacco all contain:

chemicals **(L)**, medicines **(M)**, vitamins **(N)**?

Write the letter in the grid on page 64.

If you know your stuff...

orange juice
milk
lemonade
wine
cola

...you'll spot the odd one out.

REMEMBER

Alcohol and tobacco are types of drugs. Some people who have large quantities every day are addicts. They feel ill if they don't have their drug.

On your toes What part of the body is most likely to be damaged by tobacco?

Revise wise

Leaves make their own food using energy from the sun – this is called photosynthesis.

This will help...

A leaf is the 'food factory' of a plant.

A leaf is where the plant makes its food. It uses sunlight energy to make sugars. Carbon dioxide from the air joins with water from the soil.

Look at how the different parts of the plant help this happen.

Did you know?

If a plant is put in a dark place to grow it will turn yellow.

Try these

1 The process by which plants make their own food is called ________ .

2 What is the name of the gas that is passed out through the leaves?

Puzzle code

The green substance inside leaves is called:

photosynthesis **(R)**, chlorophyll **(T)**, carbon dioxide **(S)**.

Write the letter in the grid on page 64.

If you know your stuff...

carbon dioxide

oxygen

water

chlorophyll

...you'll spot the odd one out.

REMEMBER

 On your toes The gas in the air that plants take in is called ________ .

Roots

Revise wise

The roots anchor the plant and take in water and nutrients.

The roots of all plants have two important jobs to do – they keep the plant firmly in one place and they take in water and important nutrients from the soil.

1 Roots anchor the plant. This means they keep the plant steady and stop it from blowing over.

2 The roots soak up water and nutrients (minerals dissolved in the soil and water) from the soil through tiny root hairs. The roots are connected to the stem. The stem has tubes inside it so the water and nutrients can travel to other parts of the plant.

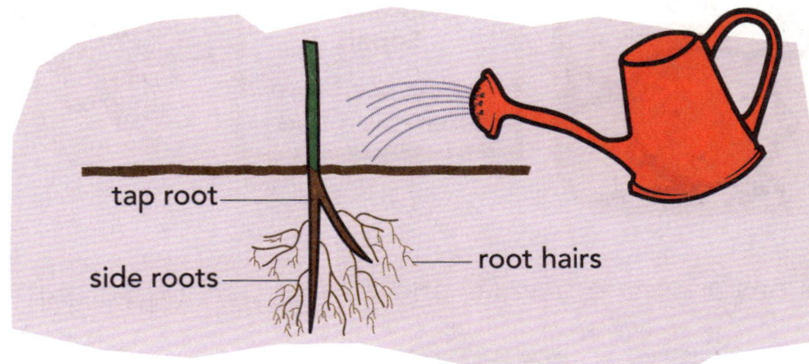

This will help...

Ships use anchors in water.
Roots anchor the plant and take in water.

Did you know?

A tree spreads its roots out three times as far as its branches.

Different types of roots

Plants have different types of roots. Some, like carrots and dandelions, have a very thick main root which is called a **tap root**. Others, like grasses, have a bundle of thin roots which spread out from the base of the stem. These are called **fibrous roots**.

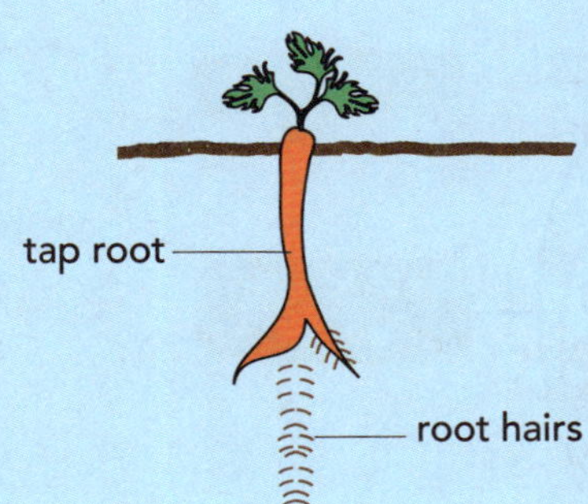

Roots need:

1 water – which is in the soil

2 nutrients – which are minerals dissolved in the soil

3 air – from air spaces in the soil.

Try these

1 The tiny roots which take in water are called root h _ _ _ _ _.

2 Plants need minerals to keep healthy. True or false?

If you know your stuff...

water

sugar

nutrients

...you'll spot the odd one out.

Puzzle code

The main, thick root of a carrot plant is called the:

root hair **(J)**, fibrous root **(K)**, tap root **(H)**.

Write the letter in the grid on page 64.

On your toes What are the two substances taken in by the roots of a plant?

Parts of a flower

Revise wise

Every flower is made up from different parts. Most flowers have male and female parts so that the plant can reproduce.

Each part of the flower has a special name and each part has a special role to play in creating new plants.

This is called **reproduction**.

This diagram shows the main parts of a flower and the special jobs they have to do.

This will help...

The stamens are the **male** part of the flower.
An **oval** is an egg shape. An **ovary** is where eggs are found.

Did you know?

The eggs of a plant are also called ovules.

Each flower has a female part (1) and a male part (2) so that new plants can be made.

1 The **carpel** is made up of:

- the **stigma** – this is sticky to catch the pollen
- the **style** – this holds up the stigma
- the **ovary** – this contains the eggs.

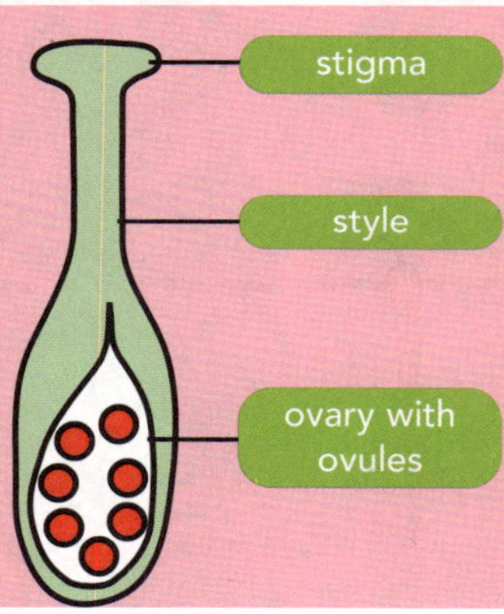

2 The **stamen** is made up of:

- the **anther** – this produces the pollen
- the **filament** – this holds the anther up.

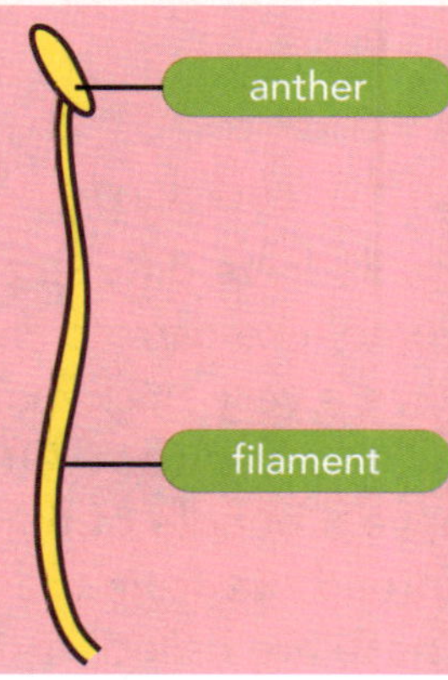

Try these

1 The carpel contains the eggs. True or false?
2 The process by which new plants are created is called ________ .

Puzzle code

Anthers:

- contain eggs **(C)**
- catch pollen **(D)**
- produce pollen **(E)**.

Write the letter in the grid on page 64.

If you know your stuff...

stamen
stigma
style

...you'll spot the odd one out.

REMEMBER

There is usually only one carpel in a flower but lots of stamens.

 On your toes What is the job of the petals?

Pollination

When pollen is taken from one plant to another it is called pollination.

Pollen from one plant has to be taken to the stigma of another plant. Pollen is often carried by insects.

1 Bees visit flowers to collect sugary nectar, which they use to make honey. When they land on the flower looking for nectar, pollen brushes off the anthers onto their legs.

2 The bee flies off to another flower to find some more nectar.

3 When the bee lands on the second flower, the pollen brushes off onto the sticky stigma.

This will help...

Pollen **s**tays on a **s**ticky **s**tigma.

Did you know?

Some plants, such as grasses and trees, are pollinated by the wind. The wind blows the long male stamens about and then carries the pollen to other plants.

Try these

1 When pollen is taken from one plant to another this is called ______________ .

2 Stamens are sticky and the pollen sticks to them. True or false?

Puzzle code

Pollination occurs when the:

- pollen goes onto the stigma **(W)**
- insects get covered in pollen **(X)**
- insects drink the nectar **(Y)**.

Write the letter in the grid on page 64.

If you know your stuff…

rain

insects

wind

…you'll spot the odd one out.

REMEMBER

Pollination usually involves two flowers – the pollen from one is taken to the stigma of the other.

On your toes Which part of the flower does the pollen stick to?

Fertilisation

Revise wise

Seeds are formed when one pollen grain joins one of the ovules in a flower – this is called fertilisation.

Once the pollen is on the stigma it is able to travel down to the ovary. A pollen grain joins together with one of the eggs or ovules. A **seed** is then formed.

This will help...

A fruit is a box with seeds. The box is made from the ovary.

Did you know?

Seeds can be as small as pepper dust or very large. – a coconut is a single seed!

Stage 1: When the pollen lands on the stigma it travels down the style. This grows down the style and into the ovule. The pollen and ovule join together to create a seed.

Stage 2: The petals begin to die and the ovary becomes bigger and bigger as the seeds grow.

Stage 3: The ovary protects the seeds inside it. It swells as the seeds grow. An ovary with seeds in is a **fruit**.

Try these

1 Joining the pollen and the egg together is called ____________ .

2 A tomato is a fruit. True or false?

Puzzle code

Fertilisation happens where:

- the pollen gets stuck to the stigma **(P)**
- the pollen and ovule join together **(O)**
- seeds start to grow **(N)**.

Write the letter in the grid on page 64.

If you know your stuff...

ovule

anther

style

...you'll spot the odd one out.

REMEMBER

pollen (male)
+
ovule (female)
=
seed

On your toes Put these processes in the order that they take place: pollination, seed formation, fertilisation.

Seed dispersal

Seeds need to move away from the parent plant – this is called seed dispersal. Disperse means 'spread about'.

This will help...

Seeds can't move on their own, they need animals, the wind or an exploding pod to help them!

Seeds need **space** to grow and therefore need to move away from the parent plant or it will become too crowded. Plants need to have plenty of light, water and room to grow.

Fruits help the seeds inside them to move away from the parent plants.

There are **three** different ways:

1 **Animals** eat fruit and then pass the seeds in droppings. Some animals, e.g. squirrels, eat hard fruits like beechnuts and acorns, and sometimes they bury them and forget where they have put them. Some fruits, e.g. burdocks, get stuck on animals' fur because they have tiny hooks all over them.

2 **The wind** disperses many fruits, e.g. sycamore wings and grass seeds.

3 **Clever tricks!** Some seeds, e.g. lupin, are in pods which **explode** when they are ripe, throwing the seeds away from the parent plant.

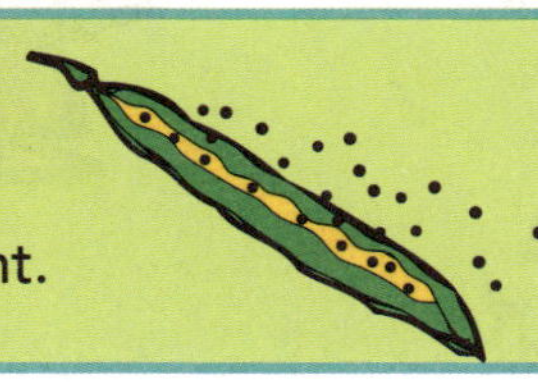

Did you know?

When a blackbird eats a blackberry, it passes the remains of the berry within 20 minutes, giving the seeds a nice coating of fertiliser!

Try these

Which method of dispersal do these seeds use?

1 lupin

2 dandelion

Puzzle code

Apple pips are dispersed by:

explosion **(M)**, wind **(P)**, animals **(R)**.

Write the letter in the grid on page 64.

If you know your stuff…

acorn

pea seed

blackberry

…you'll spot the odd one out.

REMEMBER

Seeds need to find the right conditions to germinate.

All plants grow from a seed.

On your toes What does dispersal mean?

Growing seeds

Germination is the first growth of seeds. For this to happen, seeds need water, air (oxygen) and warmth.

First, the seed coat breaks open and a tiny root appears.

The root grows down into the soil.

Then, a shoot grows upwards towards the sunlight.

Once the first leaves open, the seedling can start to make its own food.

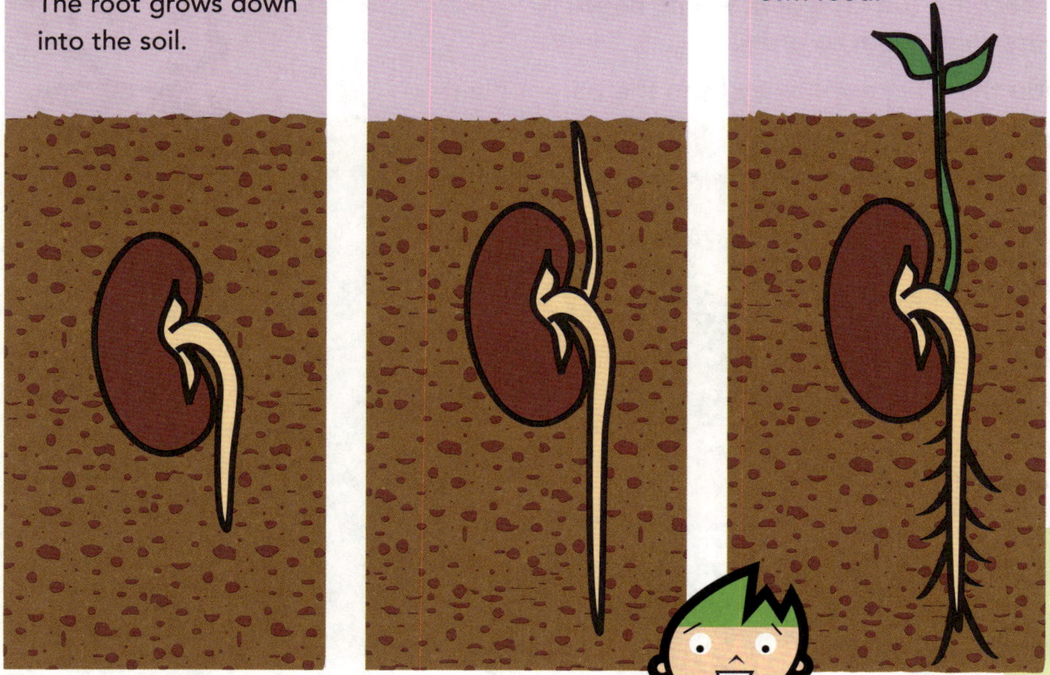

Did you know?

Many desert seeds can remain alive in the sand for 50 years or more waiting for a drop of rain.

Before the leaves are formed, the seed gets energy from its own food store.

This will help...

If there's water, warmth and air, seeds grow almost anywhere.

Try these

1 What is the first sign that a seed is beginning to germinate?

2 Seeds need energy to start to germinate. Where does this energy come from?

Puzzle code

Some seeds were sown in damp soil. After a few days they had:

- shoots but no roots **(T)**
- the beginnings of roots and many leaves **(S)**
- roots but no shoots **(K)**.

Write the letter in the grid on page 64.

If you know your stuff...

bean

grain of wheat

cabbage

...you'll spot the odd one out.

REMEMBER

Seeds will happily begin to germinate in the dark. They are usually in the soil!

 On your toes What is the name given to the first growth of a seed?

Sorting animals (1)

Revise wise

Animals are sorted into two main groups:

animals → those with backbones
animals → those without backbones.

Animals which have a backbone are called **vertebrates**.

Did you know?
All birds have wings, but not all of them can fly!

Sorting the vertebrates	Skin/body covering	How do they breathe?	How do they reproduce?	Steady inside temperature?	Other special features
Fish 	covered in scales	gills	lay eggs in water	no	have fins
Amphibians 	damp with no scales	young have gills – adults have lungs	lay eggs in water	no	adults can breathe through their skin in water
Reptiles 	dry and scaly	lungs	lay eggs on land	no	eggs have a leathery shell
Birds 	have feathers	lungs	lay eggs on land	yes	eggs have a hard, brittle shell
Mammals 	have fur or hair	lungs	give birth to live young	yes	feed babies with milk

This will help...

If the temperature of the inside of an animal stays steady, the animal can be called **warm blooded**.
Don't muddle your words.
There are lots of **animals** which are not **mammals**.

You are a mammal.
You have:
- **a body with hair**
- **a steady body temperature**
- **lungs to breath with**
- **milk to feed on as a baby.**

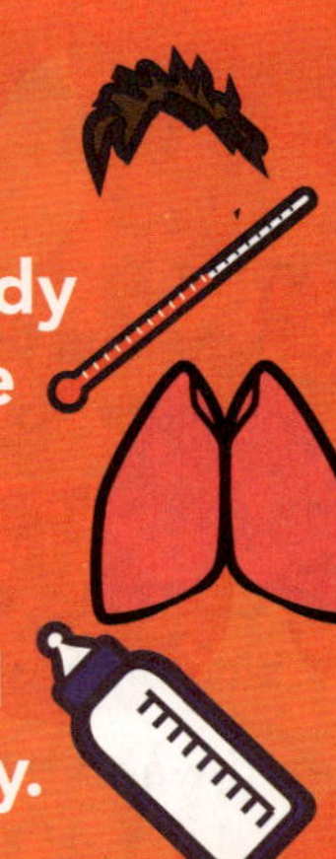

Try these

What sort of vertebrates are each of these?

1 toad
2 cod

If you know your stuff...

ostrich
sparrow
python

...you'll spot the odd one out.

Puzzle code

Which of these animals lays eggs in water:

snake **(L)**, penguin **(P)**, frog **(I)**?

Write the letter in the grid on page 64.

On your toes What kind of a vertebrate are you?

Sorting animals (2)

Revise wise

Sorting living things by looking at how they are similar or different is called classifying.

Scientist use charts, called **keys**, to help them to do this sorting. This is an example of a key that would be used to classify these five animals:

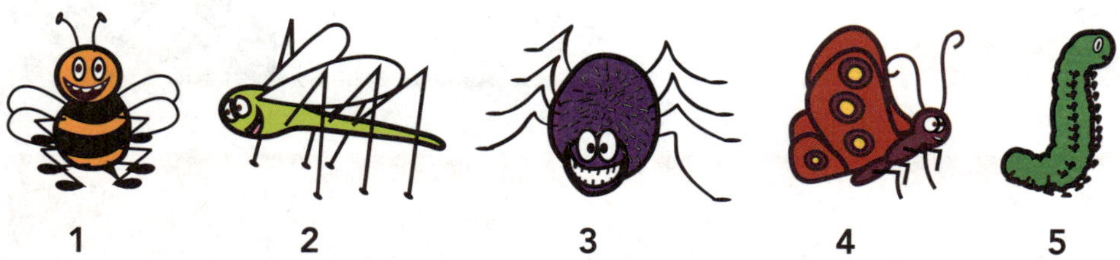

This will help...

To find out what an animal is, be a detective. The clues are in the key. Just follow the trail of questions to lead you to the answer.

Did you know?

Insects have six legs and spiders have eight. Centipedes do not really have a hundred legs – they usually have between thirty and forty.

Try these

An **invertebrate** is an animal with no backbone. Identify these invertebrates labelled 1–5 above, using the key.

Puzzle code

Which of these is not an invertebrate:

earthworm **(N)**, snail **(R)**, goldfish **(S)**?

Write the letter in the grid on page 64.

If you know your stuff...

describe

sort

classify

...you'll spot the odd one out.

REMEMBER

In a key, each question has a 'yes' or 'no' answer.

 On your toes How do you know that a woodlouse is not a kind of spider?

Plants and animals

Revise wise

The surroundings that animals or plants live in is called the environment. Different environments have different conditions – hot or cold, wet or dry, etc.

Habitats:

The hedgerow gives the blackbird shelter and a safe place to hide her nest.

Hedgerows have plenty of small creatures for birds to eat and sometimes juicy berries too.

A doorway corner gives the spider a dark, dry corner in which it can shelter, hide and build a web. It's a good place for catching insects which fly by.

Did you know?

All plants and animals have names in Latin as well as in English. Everyone in the world uses the same Latin names for each animal or plant. Often these names include the name of the person who first described the animal or plant.

This will help...

Look carefully at animals and plants. Look for clues to see how they are designed for their habitat and way of life.

Where a plant or animal lives is its habitat. How an animal or plant is suited to where it lives is called adaptation.

Adaptations:

The earthworm's body is long, pointed and slimy so it can slip through the soil.

The long legs of the crane fly can be used to balance between long blades of grass.

The body of a woodlouse is flattened so it can crawl under logs and stones. Its camouflaging grey colour helps it to hide from enemies.

Try these

1 Why does a mole have strong, thick claws?
2 Why does a polar bear have a thick fur coat?

Puzzle code

Which of these is an adaptation for hunting:

sharp claws **(D)**, long fur **(M)**, large feet **(E)**?

Write the letter in the grid on page 64.

If you know your stuff...

habitat

home

adaptation

...you'll spot the odd one out.

REMEMBER

Animals and plants get everything they need from their habitats.

On your toes Think of two ways in which a bat is adapted to hunt flying insects.

Food chains

Food chains tell us who eats what.
Food chains start with plants because they can make their own food.

Look at this food chain:

Each arrow means 'gives energy to'.
The grains of wheat give energy to the mouse.
The mouse gives energy to the barn owl.

This will help...

When you draw the arrows in a food chain, point to the eaters!

Did you know?

The largest land predator is the polar bear which grows to over 2.5 metres from nose to tail.

Don't muddle your words

You will find lots of words used to describe the members of a food chain.

Who is safe to meet?
Plant eaters are called herbivores.
Meat eaters are called carnivores.

Produce means make.
Plants are producers because they make their own food.

Consume means eat.
Herbivores and carnivores are consumers because they have to eat their food.

And finally...
Carnivores which hunt are called predators.
The animals they hunt and eat are their prey.

Chain links

You can look at several food chains and see how they join up. This is called a food web.

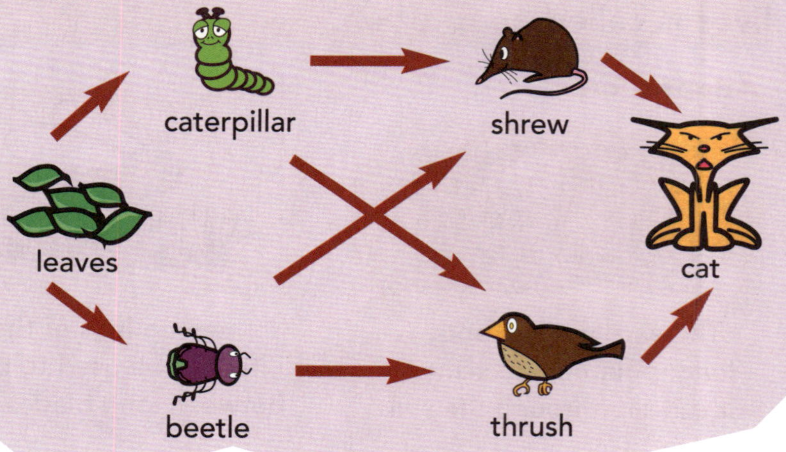

Try these

Spot the producer in each pair:
1 lettuce – rabbit
2 zebra – grass

Puzzle code

An animal which eats other animals is a:

herbivore **(E)**, producer **(F)**, predator **(O)**.

Write the letter in the grid on page 64.

If you know your stuff...

horse
tiger
cheetah

...you'll spot the odd one out.

REMEMBER

There is always a plant at the start of a food chain.

 On your toes Look at the food web above. Which animals are the herbivores and which are the carnivores?

Thinking about the environment

Revise wise

These are all able to change a habitat: weather, disease, man.

- A dry place can flood or a pond can dry up.
- Warming weather can melt frozen areas of the world.
- A disease may reduce the numbers of predators or prey in an area.
- Building and farming both change habitats.
- Dumping rubbish can harm wildlife.
- Chemical waste can poison animals and plants.
- Burning fossil fuels damages the Earth's atmosphere.

Did you know?

Over 5000 kinds of animals and 6000 kinds of plants are in danger of extinction.

This will help...

We can help the environment by:

- protecting animals and plants in danger of extinction
- recycling materials to avoid waste
- thinking of ways to save energy so less fuel is used
- taking litter home or putting it in a bin
- treating all habitats carefully.

Don't muddle your words

Pollution is the damage to habitats caused by chemicals or rubbish.

Extinction is when a kind of plant or animal dies out completely – there are no more left.

So, what happens?

If **plants** die, then there's no food or shelter for animals.

If **herbivores** die, then there's no food for predators. The habitat will change as plants are not eaten.

If **predators** die, then the number of herbivores will rise. There may not be enough plants to feed them all.

Try these

Fill in the missing words:

1 To avoid waste, we should r _ _ _ _ _ _ materials. (7 letters)

2 The damage to a habitat caused by waste is called p _ _ _ _ _ _ _ _. (9 letters)

Puzzle code

You should not drop glass bottles in the countryside because:

- a spider could build a home in it **(B)**
- broken glass is dangerous **(N)**
- glass is poisonous to some animals **(G)**.

Write the letter in the grid on page 64.

If you know your stuff...

giant panda

mountain gorilla

camel

...you'll spot the odd one out.

REMEMBER

Everything that happens to a habitat, affects the plants and animals in it.

On your toes The number of owls in an area suddenly increases – what happens to the number of field mice?

Micro-organisms

Micro-organisms are very tiny living things, which can be found just about anywhere. Like all living things, they need air to live.

Who's who?

Micro-organisms include:

Bacteria are so tiny, you could fit about 500 of them on a small full stop.

Viruses can only be seen through a powerful microscope.

Fungi can be quite large (e.g. mushrooms and toadstools), but there are microscopic fungi too.

Did you know?

Have you ever had athlete's foot? It is caused by a fungus.

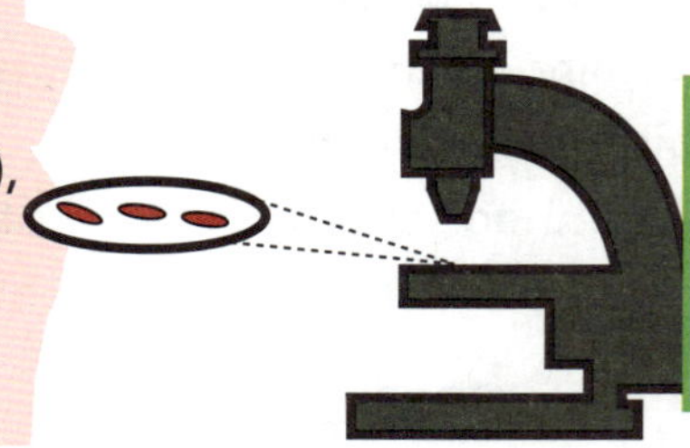

To see a **micro-organism**, you need a **microscope**.

Heroes and villains

Some micro-organisms are **useful** and some are **harmful**.

Micro-heroes

Bacteria	Turn milk to yoghurt. Help to break down dead plants and animals.
Fungi	Yeasts are fungi that are used to make bread, wine and beer. Many other fungi help to break down plants and animals.

Rogues gallery

Bacteria	Can cause food poisoning and illnesses, e.g. chest infections.
Fungi	The fungi which cause decay are useful in the garden, but aren't so welcome in the kitchen!
Viruses	Virus villains cause diseases, such as chicken pox, measles and flu.

Micro-organisms like warm, damp places and air. They will not grow well in cold or dry places. They can be killed by cooking.

This will help...

To keep harmful micro-organisms away use the **four Cs**:

- **C**lean cooking surfaces – and yourself!
- **C**over stored food.
- **C**ook food thoroughly, especially meats.
- **C**hill food in a fridge.

Try these

Which two changes might be caused by a micro-organism:

1 toast being burnt
2 a baby getting a cough
3 bread going mouldy?

If you know your stuff...

bacteria

virus

jellyfish

...you'll spot the odd one out.

Puzzle code

To help yeast to work well, you should:

cook it **(M)**, keep it warm **(E)**, put it in the freezer **(T)**.

Write the letter in the grid on page 64.

REMEMBER

Micro-organisms may be tiny but they are very important. Only some of them are harmful.

 On your toes Which micro-organism is used in bread making?

What is it made from?

Revise wise

Things are made from materials.

Some materials are natural

They come from plants and animals . . .

feathers

wood

wool

. . . or from the ground.

slate

chalk

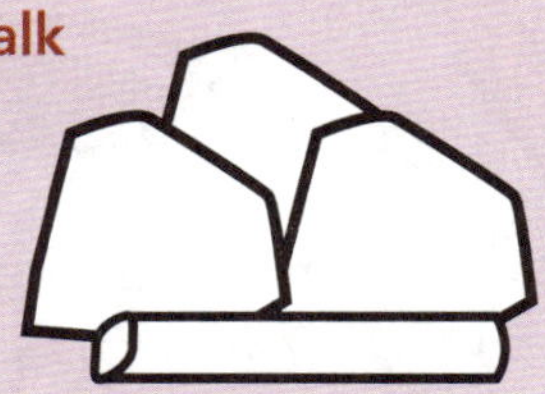

metal

Sometimes natural materials are changed or processed.

Clay is fired to make it hard.

Glass is made from sand which has been strongly heated.

Paper is made from a kind of wood 'porridge', called wood pulp.

Did you know?

The 'lead' in your pencil is not lead at all. It is made from graphite, which is a form of carbon. Diamonds are another form of carbon!

Some materials are man made

elastane

polyester

polystyrene

PVA

Man-made materials are called synthetic.

Try this

Which two of these materials are man made?
1 plastic **2** shell **3** clay **4** polystyrene

Puzzle code

What kind of cloth material is made from the cocoons of special caterpillars:

cotton **(E)**, denim **(U)**, silk **(Y)**?

Write the letter in the grid on page 64.

If you know your stuff…

wood
feathers
nylon

…you'll spot the odd one out.

REMEMBER

We can find natural materials around us, but we have to make some others.

Choosing the right material

When we are choosing a material to make something, it is important to know about its properties.

What is the material like? What does it do? These are its **properties**.

This will help...

Try to remember the word **property**. Think about all the different materials in the lost property box.

Materials can be:

hard or **soft**

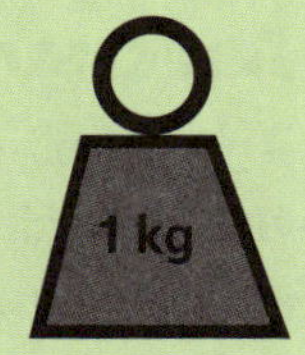

heavy or **light**

transparent or **opaque**

rough or **smooth**

flexible or **rigid**

Some materials are **waterproof** and water runs off them…

… and some are **absorbent** so water soaks into them.

Elastic materials are stretchy and they return to their starting shapes.

Some stretchy materials just stay stretched!

Did you know?

Bullet proof vests are made from a material called Kevlar.

Try these

Choose the right word to finish each sentence:

1 Glass is used to make windows because it is _____ (flexible, shiny, transparent).

2 Wood is used to make doors because it is ______ (soft, strong, stretchy).

Puzzle code

Which of these does not soak up water:

kitchen paper **(R)**, towelling **(E)**, cellophane **(O)**?

Write the letter in the grid on page 64.

If you know your stuff…

elastic

rubber band

wood

…you'll spot the odd one out.

REMEMBER

If you want to choose a material for a job you need to know about its properties.

 On your toes Flexible is another word for ____________ (stretchy, hard, bendy).

Thermal insulators and conductors

Heat always travels from hot to cold.

Heat **travels easily** through some materials, such as **metals**. These materials are **good thermal conductors**. It doesn't travel easily through other materials, such as **wood**, **cloth**, **rubber** and **plastic**. This is because they are **good thermal insulators**.

How is this useful?

Insulators keep heat in.

Insulating materials will keep warm things warm. The heat cannot escape through them.

Wrapping chips in paper helps to keep them hot.

Insulators also keep heat out.

Insulators will keep cold things cold by keeping heat away from them.

Wrapping ice cream in paper will help to keep it cold, by keeping heat out.

Did you know?

Heat can only travel through materials, including air. Vacuum flasks work by having a space where there is nothing, not even air, for the heat to travel through. This makes the best barrier of all.

This will help...

Imagine a bus conductor helping people to travel. Heat travels easily through conductors.

REMEMBER

A good insulator is a poor conductor. Think of a seesaw:

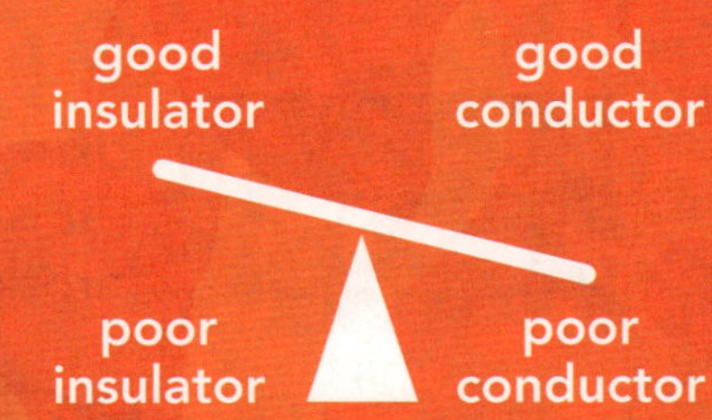

A poor insulator is a good conductor. Think of a seesaw:

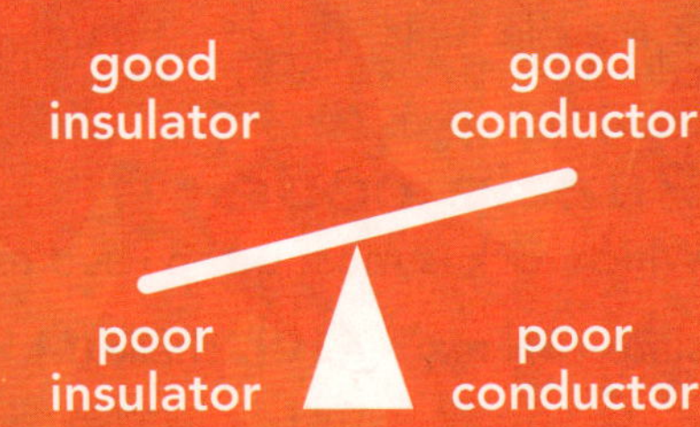

Try these

Would you use a thermal conductor or an insulator to:

1 make the bottom of a frying pan

2 cover a baby?

Puzzle code

Why is hot soup often served in a polystyrene cup?

- It keeps the soup warm **(U)**
- It helps the soup to cool quickly **(G)**
- It makes the soup taste good **(B)**.

Write the letter in the grid on page 64.

If you know your stuff…

wool

aluminium

feathers

…you'll spot the odd one out.

On your toes Why might you stir hot food in a pan with a wooden spoon not a metal one?

Rocks

**Everywhere you walk, there are rocks under the ground.
Pebbles are small pieces of rock.**

This will help...

Chat about rocks:
Colour
Hardness
Absorbency
Texture

Science rocks!

Different kinds of rock have different properties. They can be used in different ways:

Marble is hard, heavy, cool and beautifully coloured. It is also very expensive.

Chalk is a soft, white rock.

Slate breaks up into flat pieces. It is smooth and waterproof.

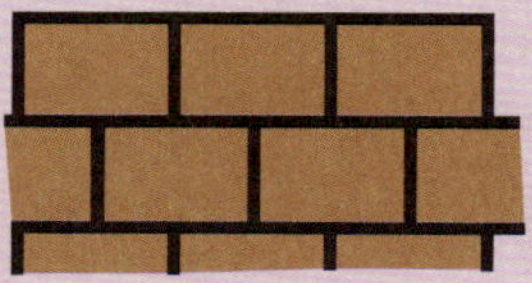

Sandstone can be cut into blocks. It has soft colours and a sandy texture (feel).

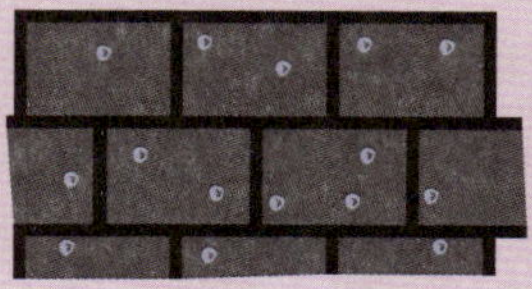

Granite is also used for building. It is hard wearing and strong. This rock sparkles with tiny crystals.

Did you know?

Chalk is made from the remains of millions of tiny sea creatures.

Don't muddle your words

Some rocks are **absorbent**. Water will soak into them.

Absorbent rocks are said to be **permeable**.

If a rock is **permeable**, it means 'water can soak through it.'

Water **cannot** soak through **impermeable** rocks.

Try these

Choose the right word to finish each sentence.

1 Slate is ________ (permeable, impermeable).
2 Marble feels ________ (warm, cool).

Puzzle code

Which rock is most often used as roof tiles:

slate **(S)**, marble **(O)**, chalk **(L)**.

Write the letter in the grid on page 64.

If you know your stuff...

absorbent
permeable
impermeable

...you'll spot the odd one out.

REMEMBER

Rocks are under the ground everywhere. There are lots of different kinds of rocks which can all be used in different ways.

 On your toes Why is chalk good for writing?

Soil

Revise wise

Soil is a mixture of:
- **tiny pieces of rock**
- **remains of dead plants and animals**
- **air**
- **water.**

Some soil has gritty grains of sand or gravel in it.

Some soil has much smaller grains of rock, called clay.

Water and soil

Bigger pieces of rock in soil let water drain through quickly. This is because the air spaces are bigger.

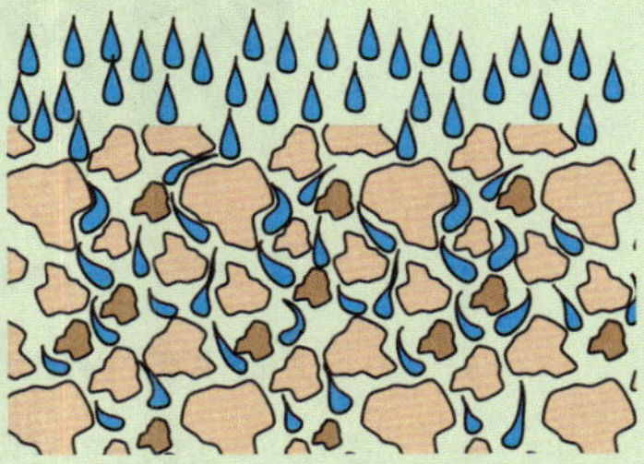

Sand and gravel grains leave spaces for water to drip through easily.

The spaces in clay soil are tiny. Water can't drip through easily, so you get lots of puddles!

This will help...

Imagine you are an ant.

Sandy soil looks like this.

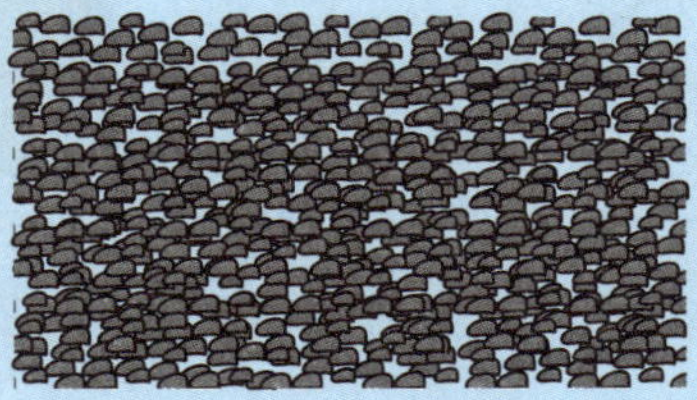

Clay soil looks like this.

Living things in the soil

Soil is full of life. There are tiny animals and larger ones, tiny plants and parts of larger ones!

The broken down remains of plants and animals in the soil is called humus.

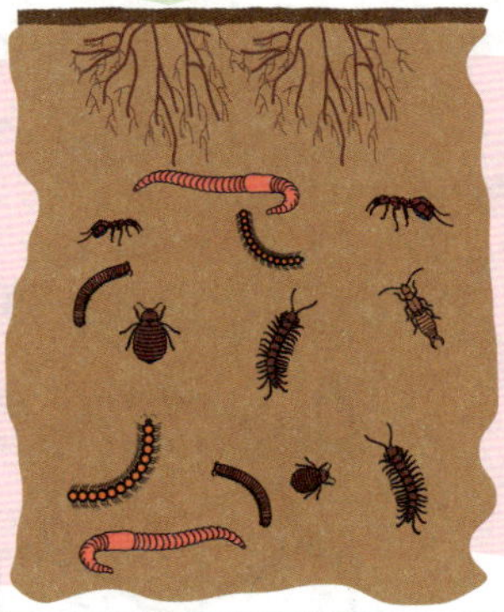

Did you know?

Many soil animals have very poor eyesight, if any at all. It is much more useful to have strong senses of touch and smell in the dark world of soil.

Try these

1 Water drains quickly through clay. True/false?
2 Animals do not live in soil. True/false?

Puzzle code

The remains of living things in the soil is called:

humans **(T)**, humus **(E)**, humorous **(N)**.

Write the letter in the grid on page 64.

If you know your stuff…

air
water
paper

…you'll spot the odd one out.

REMEMBER

There are living things in soil, and their remains, as well as rock, water and air.
Different kinds of rocks make different kinds of soil.

On your toes What kind of soil is usually muddy and covered in puddles?

Solids, liquids and gases

Revise wise

All materials are either solids, liquids or gases.
All materials are made from particles.

This will help...

Put a few dried peas or marbles on a tray. Can you make them behave like the particles in a solid, a liquid and a gas?

Solid materials have a shape.

You can hold them.

You can pour liquids.

They take up the shape of the container they are in.

You cannot usually see gases.

They spread into as much space as they can.

The particles in a solid are tightly packed, tidy and hardly move. These particles do not have much energy.

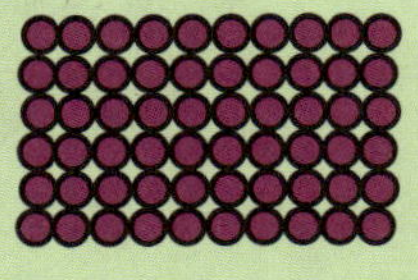

The particles in a liquid have more energy so they move around more and become less tidy and more spread out.

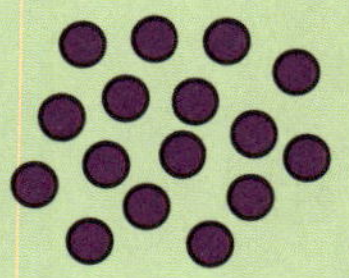

The particles in a gas are not at all tidy! They have loads of energy and they whizz about at speed spreading out into spaces.

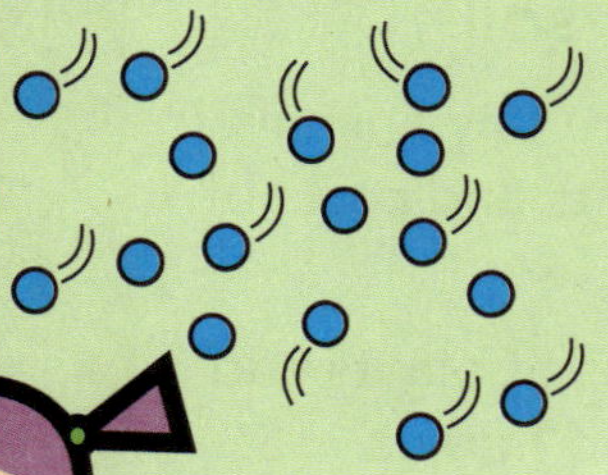

Did you know?

Sand, salt and flour can be poured but they are not liquids. If you look at them through a magnifier you will see that they are made from millions of tiny pieces of solid. Can you think of any other materials like this?

Try this

Which two of these materials are solids?

1 orange squash **3** oxygen
2 pastry **4** glass

Puzzle code

Which have the most energy:

- the particles in a gas **(E)**
- the particles in a liquid **(D)**
- the particles in a solid **(P)**?

Write the letter in the grid on page 64.

If you know your stuff...

milkshake

ice lolly

apple juice

...you'll spot the odd one out.

REMEMBER

Solids, liquids and gases are all made from particles. Particles in a solid are packed and still; particles in a gas are spread out and fast moving.

 On your toes Which has a shape of its own – a solid, a liquid or a gas?

Reversible changes

Whether materials are solids, liquids or gases, they can be changed by heating them up or cooling them down. These changes are reversible.

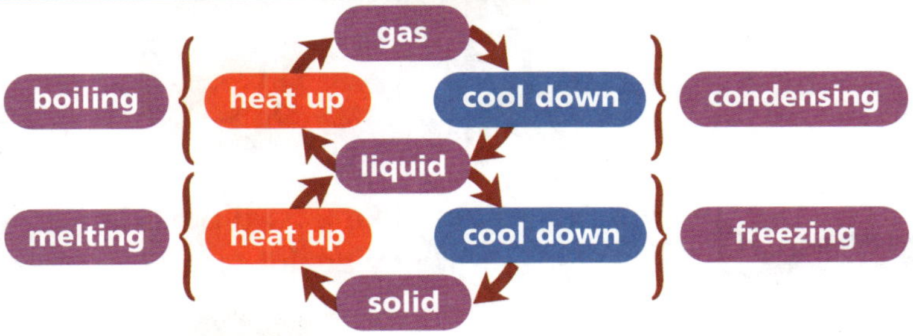

This will help...

The chart looks complicated, but think about a material you know well – water. If you warm ice it **melts**, to form liquid water. If you then put it in the freezer to cool it down, water **freezes** back to solid ice again. These changes are **reversible**.

Now, think about a kettle of **boiling** water. When liquid water gets very hot, it turns into a gas called **steam**.

Steam is **invisible** and extremely hot. When it cools down, steam turns into liquid water. This change is called **condensing**.

The water cycle

When liquid water is in a warm place with moving air, a few water particles will gradually escape from the surface. The water gradually dries up. (Think of puddles or washing drying on a sunny day.) This is called **evaporation**.

The amount of water on the planet stays pretty much the same. This happens because of the **water cycle**:

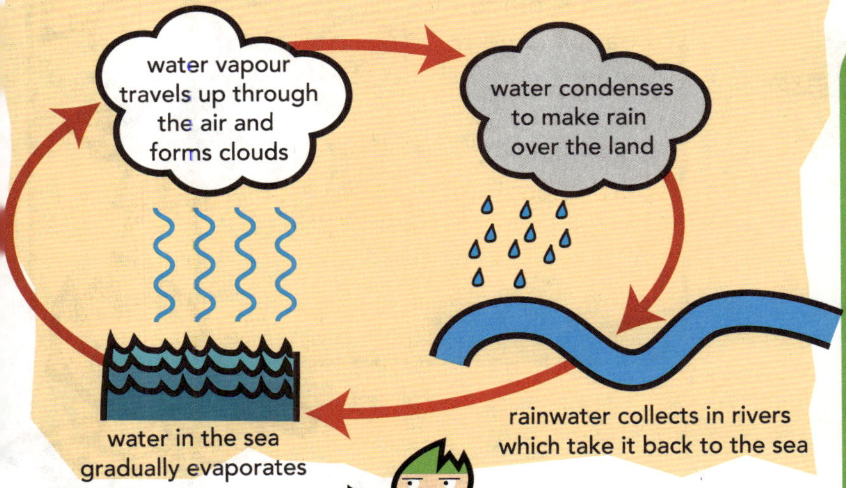

Did you know?

The **clouds** that you see when a kettle boils are not steam. The steam has cooled down and turned back to tiny drops of water which are carried in the air. This is called **water vapour**.

Try these

What is happening in each of these? Choose from: melting, freezing, boiling, condensing.

1. Chocolate is left in a warm place and goes soft.
2. You are having a hot bath. The mirror looks wet.

Puzzle code

Liquid materials freeze to solids when they are:

heated **(P)**, cooled **(H)**, stirred **(M)**.

Write the letter in the grid on page 64.

If you know your stuff...

melting
boiling
condensing

...you'll spot the odd one out.

REMEMBER

Freezing, melting, boiling and condensing are all reversible.

On your toes Why is it not a good idea to put a box of chocolates on a window sill in summer?

Changing materials: heating

Some changes caused by heat cannot be reversed. These changes are permanent.

Sometimes the structure of the material is changed – it has become a new material.

Sometimes the material burns.

These are both **chemical** changes.

Often when we cook we heat a mixture of materials. The heat makes the materials join together in new ways that cannot be undone.

This will help...

Think about your breakfast:
When you cook an egg, the egg white changes from a clear liquid to a white solid.

You can never make a hard boiled egg runny again!

Toast is really bread which has begun to burn. You can't undo toasting!

Have you ever made pancakes?

This is a chemical change too.

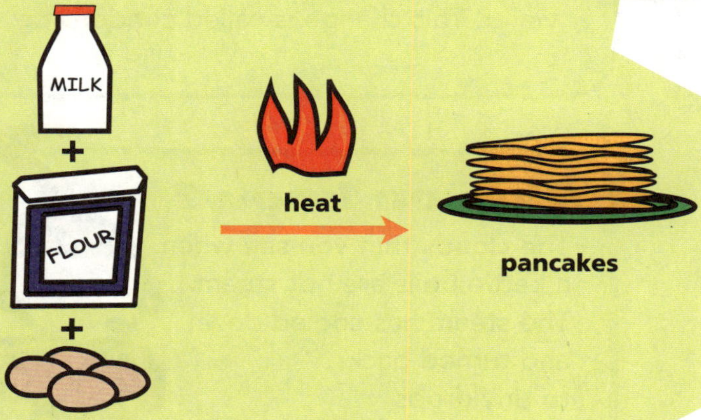

Did you know?

Glass is made by heating sand to very high temperatures. This is a permanent change!

Try these

Reversible or permanent?

1 A pond freezes over in winter. Reversible or permanent?

2 A potato is left in boiling water. Reversible or permanent?

Puzzle code

An irreversible change is one which:

- you can easily change back again **(E)**
- hasn't really happened **(I)**
- cannot be undone **(O)**.

Write the letter in the grid on page 64.

If you know your stuff...

burning

boiling

freezing

...you'll spot the odd one out.

REMEMBER

If it burns or changes into something new. This is a change you can't undo!

 On your toes What kind of change happens when water is heated – reversible or permanent?

Mixing materials

You can make mixtures by putting two or more different materials together.

You might mix two solids together:

salt +  peanuts →  salted peanuts

You can mix a **solid** with a **liquid**.

sand +  water →  wet sand

Sometimes when you mix a solid and a liquid, the solid **dissolves**. It is still there, but you cannot see it anymore.

When a solid dissolves in a liquid, the mixture is called a **solution**.

Think about putting sugar in your tea. You know the sugar is there because your tea tastes sweet, but you cannot see it.

The sugar has **dissolved** in your tea. Your tea has become a sugary **solution**.

A material which **will** dissolve is said to be **soluble**.

A material which **will not** dissolve is **insoluble**.

This will help...

The word 'solution' can also mean 'answer'.
When you solve a problem,
you find a solution.
When you dis**solve** something,
you make a **solution**.

Did you know?

Sometimes pills are soluble because it makes them easier to take. Look for the word 'soluble' on medicine packets in supermarkets.

Try these

Identify the missing words

1. When sugar is mixed with warm water, it d _ _ _ _ _ _ _ _ . (9 letters)
2. A mixture of salt and water is called a salt s _ _ _ _ _ _ _ . (8 letters)

If you know your stuff...

sand
salt
sugar

...you'll spot the odd one out.

Puzzle code

A sugar solution might be a mixture of:

sugar and salt **(Y)**, salt and water **(B)**, sugar and water **(W)**.

Write the letter in the grid on page 64.

REMEMBER

A mixture has at least two different materials in it.
When a solid dissolves in a liquid, a solution is made.

On your toes A pink powder is added to some water and disappears, but the water turns pink. What happened?

Separating mixtures

Revise wise

You can separate materials by sieving, filtering or evaporating.

Sieve to separate solid particles of different sizes.

In a solid/liquid mixture:
- if the solid has **not dissolved** use **filtering**
- if the solid has **dissolved** use **evaporation**.

This will help...

Think about sieving flour. You are separating large lumps from fine particles.

Sieves can separate solid particles of different sizes.

Filters separate insoluble solids from liquids.

Use a simple filter bed to clean muddy water.

Use filter paper to separate tiny solid particles from liquids.

When a solid – like salt or sugar – is dissolved in water, you can evaporate the liquid away to get the solid back.

Did you know?

Sieves can be made with holes of any size – large or small.

A filter is really just a kind of sieve with very tiny holes.

REMEMBER

The separation method you use depends on what you are trying to separate.
Sometimes you need: a sieve, filter paper, to use evaporation, to combine different methods.

Try these

1 How would you separate peas from sand?
2 How would you separate salt from salty water?

Puzzle code

Which of these mixtures could not be separated using a sieve?

- salt and peanuts **(J)**
- carrots and peas **(G)**
- hot milk and sugar **(S)**.

Write the letter in the grid on page 64.

If you know your stuff...

sieve

filter

shredder

...you'll spot the odd one out.

On your toes Which has bigger holes – a sieve or a filter?

Series, circuits and bulb brightness

The parts of an electrical circuit are called the components.
Different types of components can be used in circuits for different effects.

Did you know?

If you look on the metal screw of a bulb, you'll see the bulb's voltage. Make sure the voltage of all the cells in a series circuit doesn't add up to more than this or the bulb will blow!

Changing the components in a circuit can make bulbs brighter or dimmer. The switches that you use in circuits can have different effects.

If you alter a simple series circuit – one where all the components are in a line – you can affect the brightness of a bulb.

1

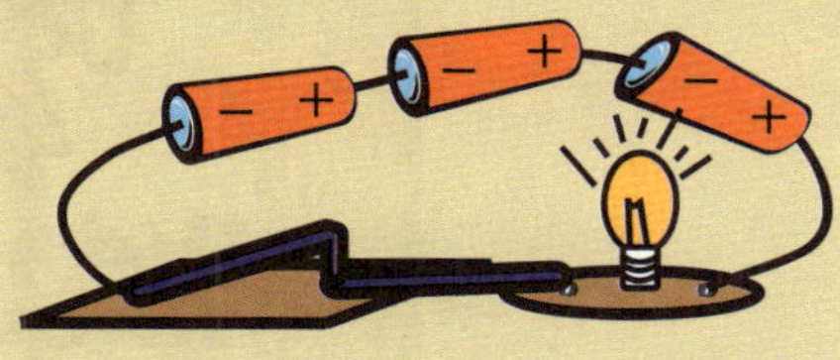

To make a bulb brighter, add more cells. But be careful – see 'Did you know?' section.

2

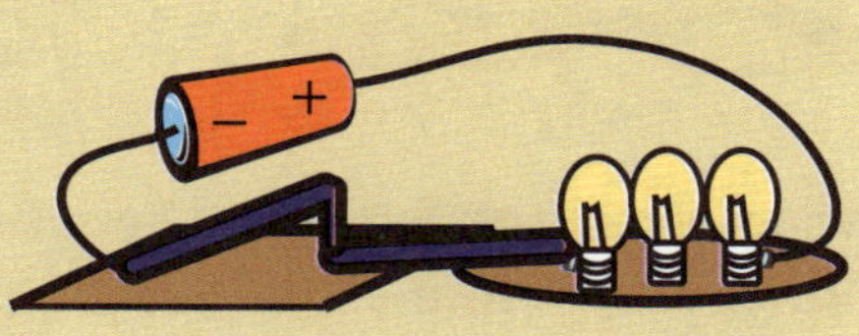

Adding more bulbs will make all the bulbs dimmer.

3

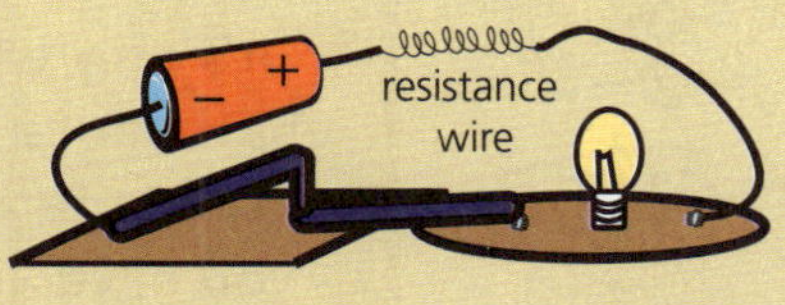

Making the wire longer will make the bulb dimmer.

4

Adding a component, e.g. a motor, will affect the brightness of a bulb in a circuit.

Different switches are used for different purposes.

This switch is good for quick switching on and off. It won't stay on unless it is pressed.

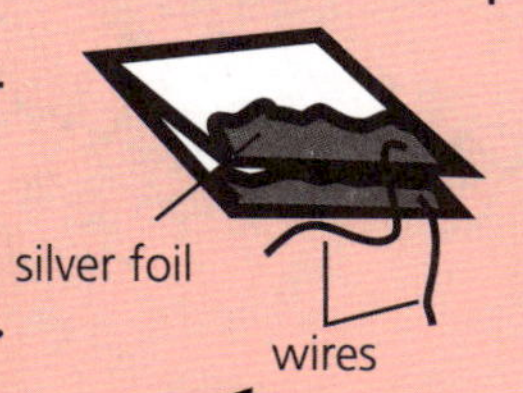

This switch can be left on.

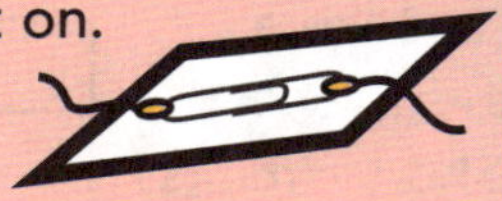

This will help...

Programmes in a TV series come one after the other. Components in a series circuit are one after the other.

Try these

1 Where would you look to find the voltage of a light bulb?
2 A circuit where all the components are in line is called a ________ circuit.

Puzzle code

To make a bulb brighter in a series circuit you could add more:

cells **(C)**, bulbs **(B)**, wire **(A)**.

Write the letter in the grid on page 64.

If you know your stuff...

bulb
switch
radio

...you'll spot the odd one out.

REMEMBER

Adding more components (parts) to a circuit will usually make bulbs dimmer.

On your toes What happens to the brightness of a bulb in a series circuit if you put a buzzer in the circuit?

Circuit diagrams

Revise wise

Circuits can be shown on paper as drawings or as diagrams.

Drawings of circuits try to show them as they really look. Circuit diagrams don't look like the real circuit – they represent circuits using symbols.

Circuit drawings and diagrams showing the same circuit look very different.

This drawing and diagram show a series circuit. Series circuits are circuits where all the working parts follow one another in a line.

How to draw circuit diagrams:

1 Know your symbols!
2 Don't leave any gaps between parts of the circuit.
3 Use straight lines to draw wires, with right-angled corners.

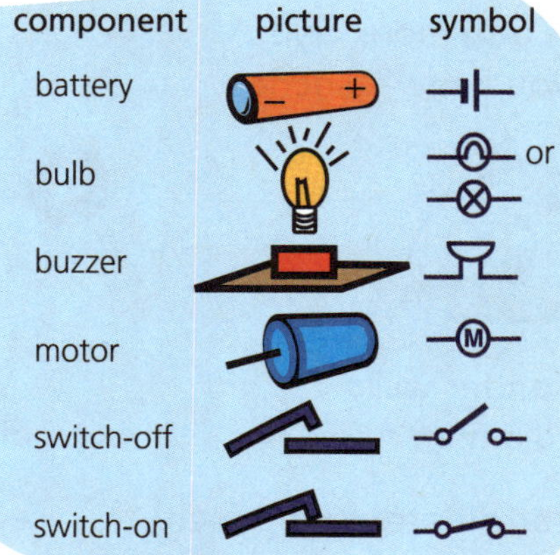

Short circuit!

This circuit allows the electricity to take a short cut (the dotted line). There is a 'short circuit', so the bulb won't light. Short circuits damage cells!

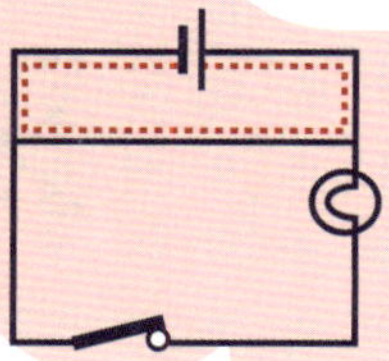

Try these

1 The symbol for a motor is an M in a circle. True or false?
2 How should you draw wires in circuit diagrams?

Puzzle code

When drawing circuit diagrams, you should try not to put which of the following between wires and components:

gaps **(I)**, short circuits **(G)**, series **(U)**.

Write the letter in the grid on page 64.

This will help...

Think about keeping circuit diagrams simple. Don't have wires crossing over each other in your drawing.

Did you know?

What we often call a 1.5 V battery is called a **cell** by scientists. It's only when you have more than one cell together that you have a **battery**.

REMEMBER

When drawing circuit diagrams, try to use the symbols shown on this page. Make sure there are no gaps between wires and components, and draw wires as straight lines with right-angled corners.

If you know your stuff…

buzzer

…you'll spot the odd one out.

 On your toes Short circuits are good because they save electricity. True or false?

Forces: pushes and pulls

Forces are pushes and pulls.
Upthrust is a force pushing up.

All forces are either pushes or pulls.

Upthrust is a force pushing up in water and air, but it is much greater in water than in air.

Did you know?

For any object to float – even a huge ship – upthrust has to equal the force of gravity pulling down.

Forces can have many effects. They can make things:

speed up

slow down

change direction

change shape

If you push or pull something, you'll feel a resisting push or pull. This is called an 'opposing' force. Sometimes the push or pull back will be small and sometimes it will be big.

Forces can act without anything happening (see page 38).

Things weigh less when you put them in water. This is because the water pushes up and cancels out some of the force of gravity pulling down. This push up from the water is called **upthrust**.

Sometimes upthrust equals the force of gravity pulling down…

… and sometimes it doesn't!

Try these

1 When forces are in action, they always make something move. True or false?
2 Upthrust acts in opposition to ________ .

Puzzle code

For an object to float, upthrust and the force of gravity must:

- act in the same direction **(J)**
- be equal **(E)**
- act downwards **(M)**.

Write the letter in the grid on page 64.

If you know your stuff…

speed up
change colour
change direction

…you'll spot the odd one out.

REMEMBER

A force is a push or a pull. When something is in water, gravity pulls it down and upthrust pushes it up.

On your toes A force is a ________ or a ________ .

Forces: acting in opposition

Revise wise

When things are pushed or pulled, an opposing push or pull can be felt.

When one force acts, another force acts in the **opposite direction**. If things don't start to move, the forces are balanced. If things start to move, speed up, slow down or change direction, the forces are unbalanced.

There are several ways in which pushes and pulls can be **balanced** (where the forces at work are equal).

This will help...

When forces are balanced there is no movement. Think of a tug-of-war game. If the two teams are balanced, the rope will not move.

Did you know?

Ships float higher up in salt water than they do in fresh water, because salt water gives more upthrust.

When things start to move, speed up, slow down or change direction, then the forces are **unbalanced** (one force is bigger than another).

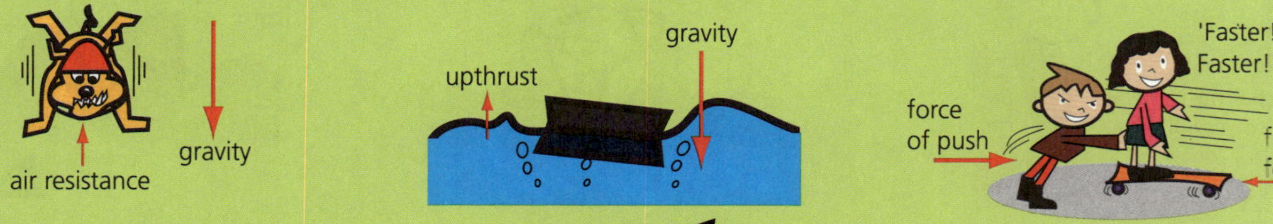

Try these

1 When forces are ________________ , things start to move.
2 When forces are ________________ , things stay still.

Puzzle code

When you push or pull something, you can:

- feel an opposing push or pull **(N)**
- feel an extra force helping you **(K)**
- feel nothing **(H)**.

Write the letter in the grid on page 64.

If you know your stuff…

gravity
upthrust
energy

…you'll spot the odd one out.

REMEMBER

If you push or pull something, you'll feel a pull or push in the opposite direction. Sometimes things will move and sometimes they won't, but there are always two forces working, not just one.

 On your toes What is name of the force which pushes up in water?

Forces: gravity

Revise wise

Gravity is a force that pulls objects down towards the Earth.

Gravity is a force that acts between objects. On Earth, gravity pulls things down towards the centre of the Earth.

Gravity is one of the forces that scientists call 'mysterious'. It is the force of attraction that pulls all objects on Earth towards the centre of the Earth and stops them flying off into space.

Gravity pulls objects towards the Earth's centre.

An Earth without gravity.

This will help...

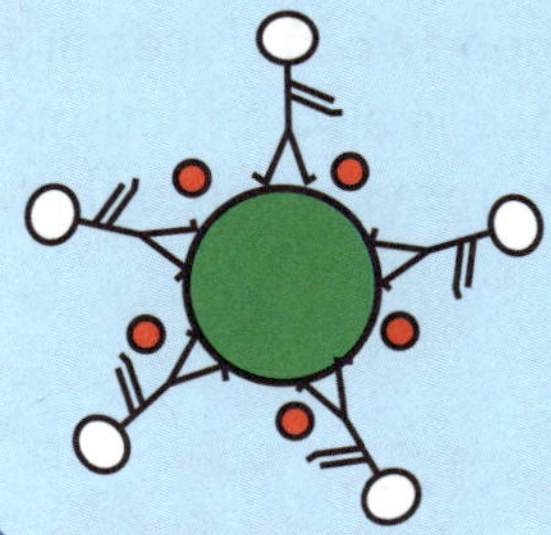

It doesn't matter where you are, gravity causes things to fall towards the centre of the Earth.

Did you know?

The moon is smaller than the Earth, so the force of gravity is less on the moon than it is on the Earth. Because gravity gives objects weight, you would weigh less on the moon than you do on Earth.

Because of gravity, all objects on Earth have **weight**. Wherever you are on Earth, you will weigh roughly the same. Way out in space, away from any gravitational force, you would weigh nothing.

You can't beat gravity, but sometimes it seems like you have:

See page 37.

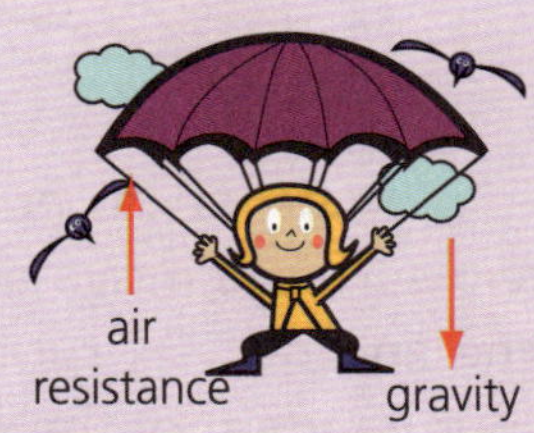

See page 40.

Try these

1 There are some places on Earth where you don't feel the effects of gravity. True or false?
2 The sun is much, much bigger than the Earth. Do you think the sun has a stronger or a weaker gravitational force than the Earth?

Puzzle code

Gravity is a force of:

- repulsion between two objects **(E)**
- friction between surfaces **(F)**
- attraction between two objects **(C)**.

Write the letter in the grid on page 64.

If you know your stuff...

a pull to the centre of the Earth

gravity

a push away from the Earth

...you'll spot the odd one out.

Gravity is a force of attraction between objects. The Earth is a huge object, and pulls all smaller objects on it towards its centre.

On your toes Gravity pulls objects towards the ________ of the Earth.

Friction and air resistance

Friction is a force that acts to oppose movement.

Friction happens when two surfaces are in **contact** with one another. Air resistance is also a frictional force, as air acts to slow things down that are moving through it.

When something moves across a surface, frictional force between the two surfaces slows down the moving object.

Rough surfaces slow things down quickly. Smoother surfaces don't slow you down as quickly.

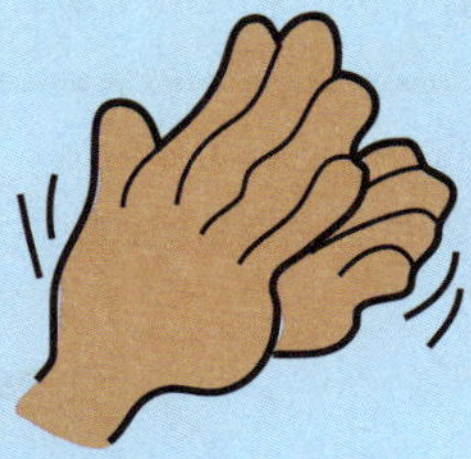

Friction produces heat as two surfaces move across one another. Try rubbing your hands together – they get warm!

Because air is made of gases, it slows you down as you move through it. Things with a large **surface area** move through the air slowly. More **streamlined** objects move through the air more quickly.

This will help...

When people 'rub each other up the wrong way' we say there is friction between them!

Did you know?

Without friction there would be no grip in the world. Our feet would slide all over the place. The slightest touch on any object would move it, and it would keep moving until it bumped into something else.

Try these

1 What does friction oppose?

2 Rougher surfaces slow things down better than smooth surfaces. True or false?

Puzzle code

Air resistance slows things down when you move, and friction acts when things:

separate **(J)**, touch **(E)**, fall **(M)**.

Write the letter in the grid on page 64

If you know your stuff…

friction

air resistance

streamlining

…you'll spot the odd one out.

REMEMBER

Friction is a force that acts to slow things down. It is a contact force that acts between surfaces.

 On your toes What gives us grip when we walk?

Size and direction of forces

Revise wise

We can measure forces, describe how big they are and explain the direction they move in.

Forces can be big or small and they always act in a particular direction. If you're describing a force, it is important to give its size and direction.

Forces are measured in **newtons (N)**. We can use a **newton meter** to find out the size of a force. For example, if you pull a rock along the ground, you can hook a newton meter to the rock and read how much force you are using to pull it.

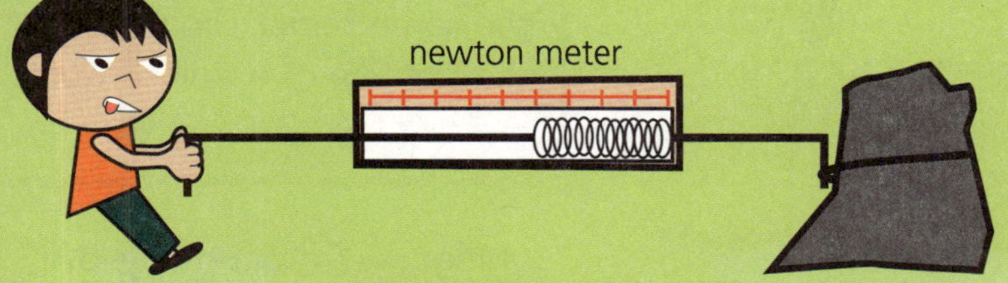

This will help...

We can't see forces working. Drawing arrows helps us to think about their size and direction.

Did you know?

Forces can't be seen, but you can see the effects of a force. When a force is acting, something will be starting to move, stopping, speeding up, slowing down, changing direction or changing shape.

Arrows can be used to show the direction and size of a force.

Using a small force to move an object.

Using a large force to move an object.

It's important to remember that forces can act in many directions at once.

Try these

You use your finger to push a pencil sharpener across a desk.

1. When you draw what's happening, do you use a large or small arrow to show the force you are using?
2. In what direction would you draw the arrow?

Puzzle code

When describing a force, it is important to give:

- the size of the force only **(C)**
- the size and direction of the force **(I)**
- the direction of the force only **(V)**.

Write the letter in the grid on page 64.

If you know your stuff…

a large number of newtons

a large arrow

a small force

…you'll spot the odd one out.

REMEMBER

When thinking about forces, it's important to give their size (by measuring in newtons or by drawing arrows). It's also important to give their direction (the best way to do this is to draw arrows).

On your toes All drawings showing forces in operation have only one arrow in them. True or false?

Magnets

Revise wise

Magnets attract some metal objects, and can attract and repel one another.

There is a force of **attraction** between magnets and metals that have some **iron** in them. Magnets can attract one another, but they can also push one another away (**repel** one another).

Magnetism is a force that even scientists call 'mysterious'.

The ends of a magnet are called the **North and South poles** of the magnet. If you hold the ends of two magnets together, you will quickly be able to see that two poles that are the same will repel one another. However, you will also discover that a North and a South pole will attract one another.

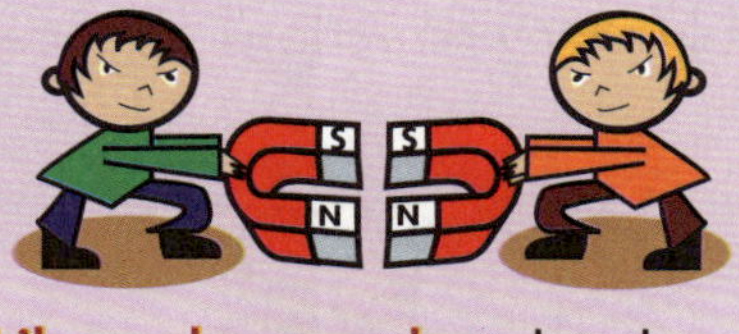

Like poles repel each other.

Unlike poles attract each other.

This will help...

Attract means 'pull towards'.
Repel means 'push away'.
Insect **repel**lent makes insects **go away**!

Did you know?

Magnetic forces can act through solids and liquids. A strong magnet can move a steel paper clip through many sheets of paper, or lift the same paper clip up from the bottom of a sink of water.

Magnets attract many, but not all, metal objects. For a magnet to attract a metal object, the object must be made of an **iron-based metal** (iron, steel, stainless steel).

Attracted by a magnet? Iron based?

Try these

1 The North pole of a magnet will repel the North pole of another magnet. True or false?
2 What metals are attracted to magnets?

Puzzle code

If a North pole of one magnet is put near the South pole of another magnet:

- they will attract one another **(S)**
- they will repel one another **(B)**
- they will turn into iron **(L)**.

Write the letter in the grid on page 64.

If you know your stuff...

iron nail
paper clip
wooden spoon

...you'll spot the odd one out.

REMEMBER

Magnets can attract and repel each other. Magnets attract iron-based metal objects.

 On your toes What are the ends of a magnet called?

Light and shadows

Revise wise

Light travels from a source, often causing shadows to be formed.

Some materials will let light pass through, but many objects block the light and this leads to shadows being formed.

Light comes from primary sources that emit (give out) light. Light travels in straight lines.

Primary sources of light

When light hits a solid object, two main things happen. Light is reflected in all directions, allowing us to see the object (see page 45). The object also blocks the light, causing shadows to be formed.

The length of the shadow formed depends upon the position of the light source.

Did you know?

Because light travels in straight lines, the shadow of an object will be the same shape as the object. However, shadows are often not sharp-edged. They often have fuzzy edges because light is coming from a spread-out source, or from several sources at once.

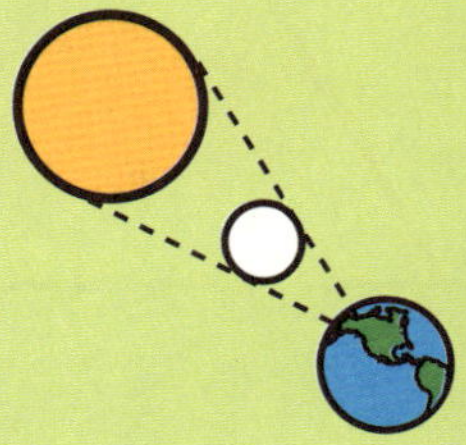

During an eclipse of the sun, the moon passes between the sun and the Earth and causes a shadow on part of the Earth's surface. For more about the movement of the Earth and moon, see page 49.

Don't muddle your words

Some materials let light through easily. These are **transparent** materials. Some materials let some light through. These are **translucent** materials. Some materials let no light through. These are **opaque** materials.

This will help...

A classroom window is transparent. A bathroom window is translucent. A wooden door is opaque.

Try these

1 Light can bend round objects. True or false?
2 Shadows change when the source of light moves. True or false?

Puzzle code

Sometimes the moon causes a shadow to fall on the Earth. We call this:

an eclipse **(G)**, a fuzzy shadow **(N)**, a light source **(B)**.

Write the letter in the grid on page 64.

If you know your stuff...

cellophane

sunglasses

blindfold

...you'll spot the odd one out.

REMEMBER

Light travels from a source. Solid objects block the light causing shadows to be formed.

On your toes An object is moved nearer to a light source. Will its shadow become larger or smaller?

Mirrors

Revise wise

Light is reflected directly from shiny surfaces.

All surfaces reflect light, scattering it in all directions. Mirrors are a bit different – they are shiny surfaces that reflect light in **predictable** ways.

If you shine a light on a flat mirror, it will bounce off the mirror at the same angle, but in the opposite direction.

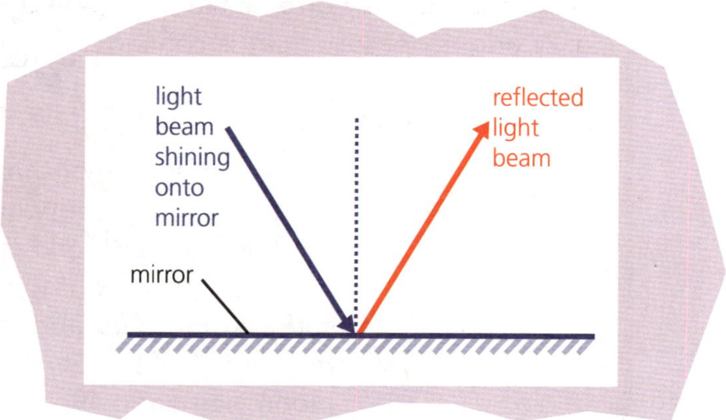

You can use this idea to re-direct torch light.

This will help...

If the ground is smooth, you can predict how a ball will bounce. This is like light bouncing on a flat shiny mirror.

Did you know?

Mirrors which curve inwards can make upside-down reflections. Look into the 'bowl' of a shiny spoon to see this.

If you look at an image in a mirror, it will seem to be the same distance behind the mirror as the object is in front of it.

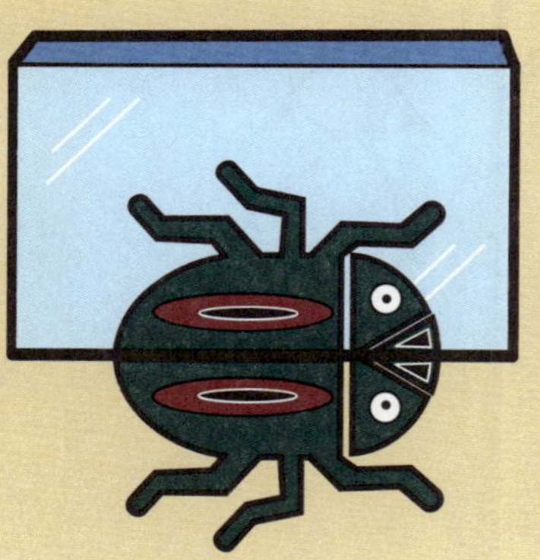

Try these

1. If a beam of light hits a flat mirror, you can't tell where it will be reflected. True or false?
2. You sometimes see an upside-down image in a flat mirror. True or false?

Puzzle code

The image we see in a mirror is called a:

reflection **(O)**, reaction **(G)**, shadow **(Y)**.

Write the letter in the grid on page 64.

If you know your stuff...

reflection

shadow

mirror image

...you'll spot the odd one out.

REMEMBER

Mirrors reflect light in predictable ways. If you shine a light on a mirror, you should be able to say in which direction the light will be reflected.

 On your toes Mirrors reflect light in ways that are ________.

Eyes and vision

Revise wise

We see things when light from them enters our eyes.

Some objects emit (give out) light. Light is reflected off all other objects. When this light enters our eyes, we are able to see objects.

Not many of us have experienced total darkness – when there is no light at all. In total darkness it's impossible to see anything at all.

This will help...

Light travels in straight lines. Always draw light as straight arrows.

Did you know?

The coloured part of the eye (the **iris**) can open and close to control the amount of light that enters the eye. In a dark room, the iris will open to let in more light. The window in the middle of the iris is called the **pupil**.

Eyes are amazing things. They are designed to allow us to see light in two ways:

1 light coming directly from light sources

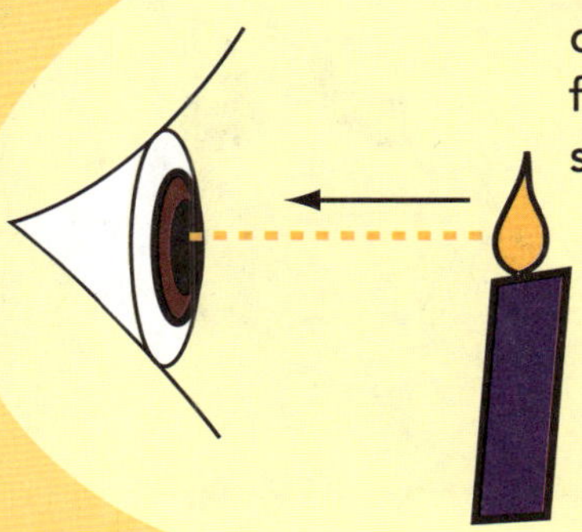

2 light reflected off an object.

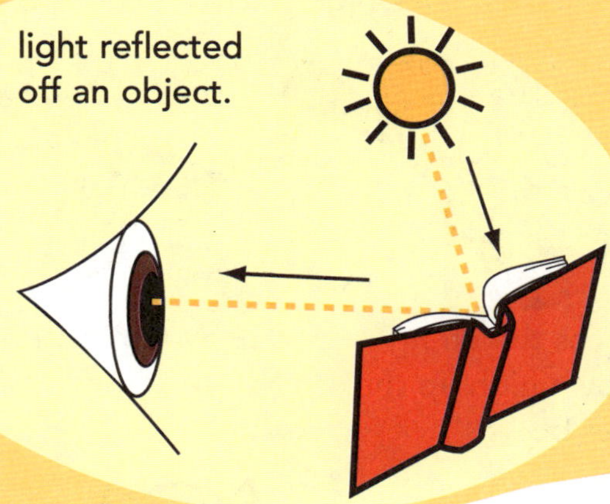

Try these

1 We see objects when light from them enters our eyes. True or false?
2 If you look very hard in total darkness, it is possible to see some things. True or false?

Puzzle code

Light travels in:

wavy lines **(K)**, zigzag lines **(A)**, straight lines **(O)**.

Write the letter in the grid on page 64.

If you know your stuff...

iris

pupil

child

...you'll spot the odd one out.

REMEMBER

Without light, you wouldn't be able to see anything.

On your toes What must enter your eyes if you're going to see anything?

Sounds and vibrations

Revise wise

All sounds happen because something is vibrating.

Sound is a kind of energy caused by vibrations, and sometimes the vibrations that make sounds can't be seen. The **pitch** and **loudness** of sounds change depending on the size of the vibrations making the sounds. Loud sounds carry more energy that quiet sounds. Slow vibrations produce low sounds, fast vibrations produce high sounds.

Loudness has a scientific name – **volume**. Soft, quiet sounds are caused by small vibrations. Loud sounds are made by large vibrations.

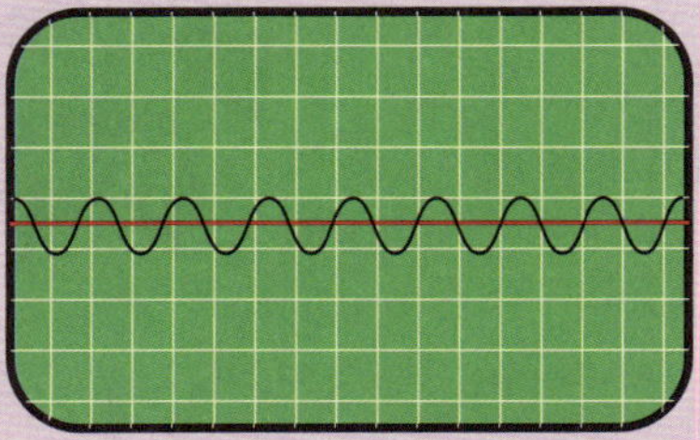

Sound waves from a soft sound

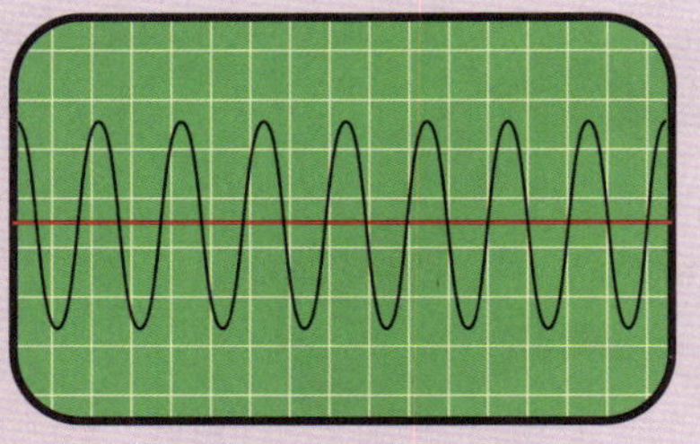

Sound waves from a loud sound

Sounds are not only loud or soft, they also have a high or low **pitch**. High pitched notes are caused when a sound source vibrates quickly and low pitched sounds are made when the sound source vibrates slowly. To make high pitched sounds on a guitar:

Press the string down high up the fret board

Play a thin string

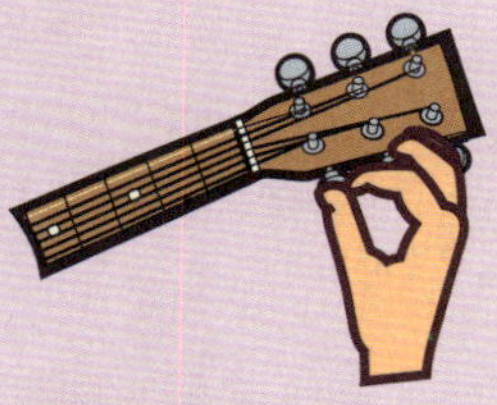

Tighten the string

This will help...

The **longer** the string or air column, the **lower** the note.

Did you know?

The human ear is remarkable. You can hear sounds made by sources that are vibrating very slowly (20 vibrations a second). You can also hear sounds made by sound sources that are vibrating very quickly (20 000 vibrations a second!).

Try these

1 Only big vibrations make sounds. True or false?

2 What is the scientific word for loudness?

Puzzle code

To make a high-pitched sound on a guitar string:

- play a thick string **(Z)**
- play a thin string **(D)**
- loosen the string **(T)**.

Write the letter in the grid on page 64.

If you know your stuff…

loudness

volume

pitch

…you'll spot the odd one out.

REMEMBER

Sound is energy caused by vibrations and needs something to travel through.

 On your toes What kind of vibrations make loud sounds?

Hearing

Sounds need a medium to travel through.

To hear sounds, the vibrations from sound sources need to travel through a medium. Then they travel to the ear. Sounds travel through many different mediums, such as metal, water, air – in fact, they travel through all solids, liquids and gases.

Solids

Liquids

Gases

This will help...

Think of a dropping a stone into a pond. Ripples travel away from the stone in circles. The vibrations from a sound source travel outwards like this in all directions.

Did you know?

No sound can be heard in space. That's because there's no atmosphere, so there is no gas for sounds to travel through.

Sometimes we want to stop the sounds reaching our ears so we use an **insulator**. These are materials that are not very good at letting sounds through.

REMEMBER

It's only when sound waves enter the ear that we hear them. Without an ear drum that can vibrate, you wouldn't be able to hear the sound waves that come to you through the air.

Try these

1 Sounds travel through space. True or false?
2 Sounds travel well through insulators. True or false?

Puzzle code

Sounds travel through:

- solids only **(G)**
- solids, liquids and gases **(F)**
- solids and liquids only **(S)**.

Write the letter in the grid on page 64.

If you know your stuff…

wood

metal

water

space

…you'll spot the odd one out.

The Earth and the moon

Revise wise

The Earth orbits the sun, and the moon orbits the Earth. The sun, moon and Earth are all roughly spherical.

The Earth takes a year to **orbit** (move right around) the sun, and the moon takes about 28 days to orbit the Earth.

The Earth moves around the sun in an elliptical (oval) orbit.

The moon reflects the sun's rays, and we see it best in the night sky.

The Earth is tilted on its axis. Because of this, at different points on its journey around the sun some parts of the Earth – like Britain – have different seasons.

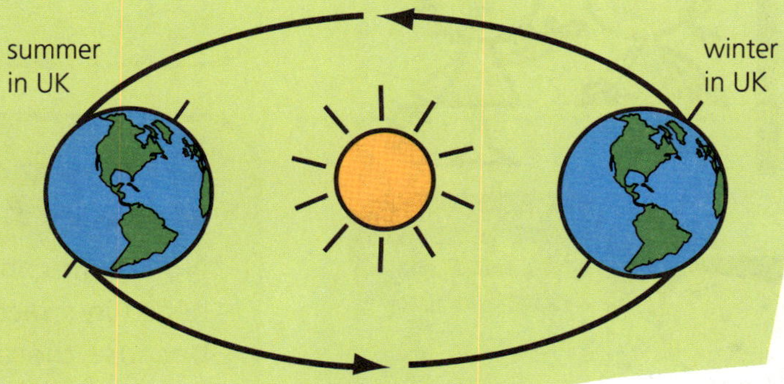

Only one side of the moon is lit by the sun. Because the moon orbits the Earth, we see different amounts of the side lit by the sun at different times. That's why the moon seems to change shape in the sky over roughly 28 days.

Sometimes only the dark (unlit) side of the moon faces the Earth. Then there seems to be almost no moon in the sky – we say that there's a 'new moon'.

This is how the moon looks to us at different times as it orbits the Earth:

Did you know?

The sun's gravitational pull is what keeps the Earth in orbit around it. Similarly, the Earth's gravitational pull holds the moon in its orbit around the Earth.

Try these

1 The moon orbits the Earth roughly every ________ days.

2 What force allows the Earth to orbit the sun, and the moon to orbit the Earth?

Puzzle code

When the dark side of the moon is facing the Earth so that we can't see it, we call this a:

full moon **(H)**, half moon **(Q)**, new moon **(U)**.

Write the letter in the grid on page 64.

If you know your stuff…

365¼ days

1 month

time for the Earth to orbit around the sun

…you'll spot the odd one out.

REMEMBER

The Earth is tilted and orbits the sun over one year. Because of these two things, Great Britain and other parts of the Earth have different seasons.

 On your toes What shape are the sun, the Earth and the moon? (Be careful!)

The Earth's movements

Shadows change as the sun appears to move in the sky.

The Earth spins on its axis and because of this makes the sun seem to move in the sky.

The sun doesn't move, we do!

Did you know?

The sun has a diameter of 1.5 million kilometres and is 150 million kilometres from the Earth!

The Earth spins on its axis (an imaginary line drawn through the centre of the Earth from the North to the South Pole). It takes 24 hours to completely rotate. For the side of the Earth that's lit by the sun, it's daytime. For the side that isn't facing the sun, it's night.

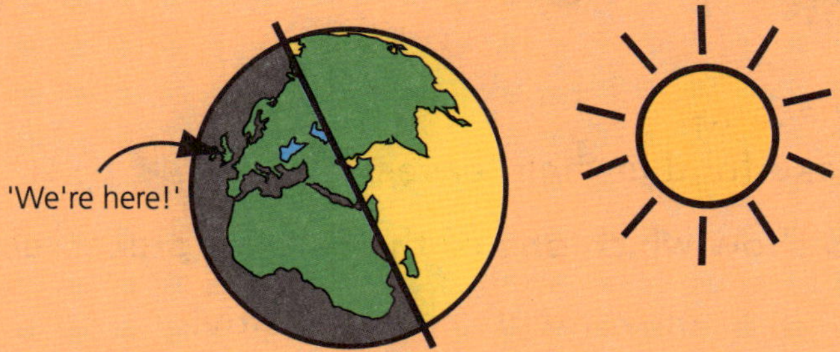

The sun seems to be moving in the sky because the Earth is rotating.

At sunrise, the sun comes into view as the Earth spins towards it. Shadows are long because the sun is low in the sky.

At midday, shadows are short because the spin of the Earth has moved us to face the sun directly. The sun is high in the sky.

At dusk, shadows are long again as we spin away from the sun and it seems to sink low in the sky.

Try these

1 The spinning of the sun is what makes day and night happen. True or false?
2 Why are there long, west-facing shadows in the early morning?

Puzzle code

At midday, shadows are:

- at their shortest **(N)**
- quite long **(R)**
- at their longest **(P)**.

Write the letter in the grid on page 64.

If you know your stuff…

shadows move during the day

the Earth moves during the day

the sun moves during the day

…you'll spot the odd one out.

The sun doesn't move. It is the spinning of the Earth that makes the sun seem to move across the sky.

Test questions

Revise wise

1 Squirrels eat acorns.
Oak trees make food in their leaves.

Tick a box to show which one of the five life processes is described in these sentences.

☐ growth ☐ movement ☐ sensitivity ☐ nutrition ☐ reproduction

2 Emily has just been to the dentist and has had two fillings. She doesn't understand why this has happened because she cleans her teeth when she gets up every morning before she has her breakfast.

a When should Emily clean her teeth?

____

b Why?

____

3 Fill in the missing words.

a The **brain** controls the whole body by sending ______________________ .

b The **heart** ______________________ blood around the whole body.

c The **kidneys** ______________________ the blood by removing waste substances and make urine which is stored in the bladder.

4 Rita had just won a race at her school's sports day. She noticed that her body has changed since she started the race. She was panting and sweating.

What other changes did she notice? Write them in the boxes.

She was panting.

She was sweating.

5 Use these words to fill in the spaces in the sentences below:

relaxed   hard   soft   contracts   relaxed   contracts

a Arm lifting

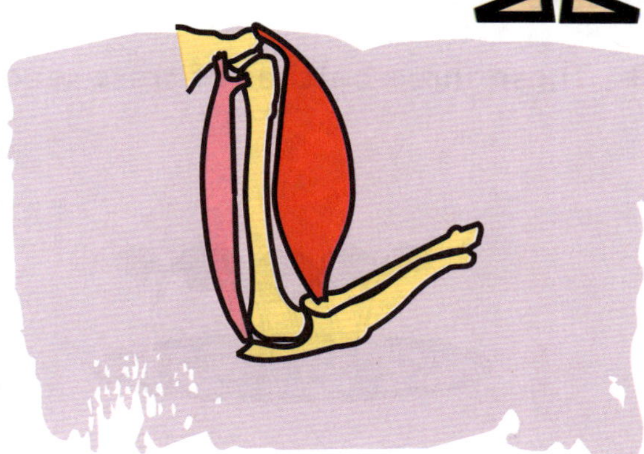

When you lift your forearm, your biceps muscle

_________________________ ; it becomes

thicker and feels _________________________ .

At the same time, your triceps muscle is

_________________________ .

b Arm straight

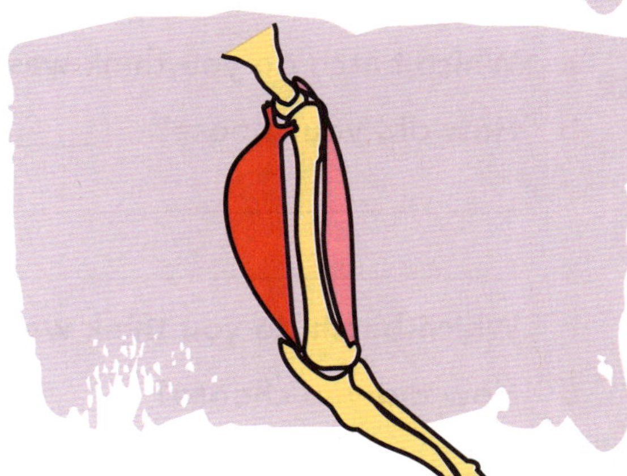

When you straighten your arm, your biceps

muscle is _________________________ and

feels _________________________ .

At the same time, your triceps muscle

_________________________ .

6 Plants are different from animals because they can make their own food.

This process is called photosynthesis.

a Can plants carry out photosynthesis at night time?

b Explain your answer.

____

____

7 A flower has some parts which are male and some which are female. label the female parts 'F' and the male parts 'M' in this diagram.

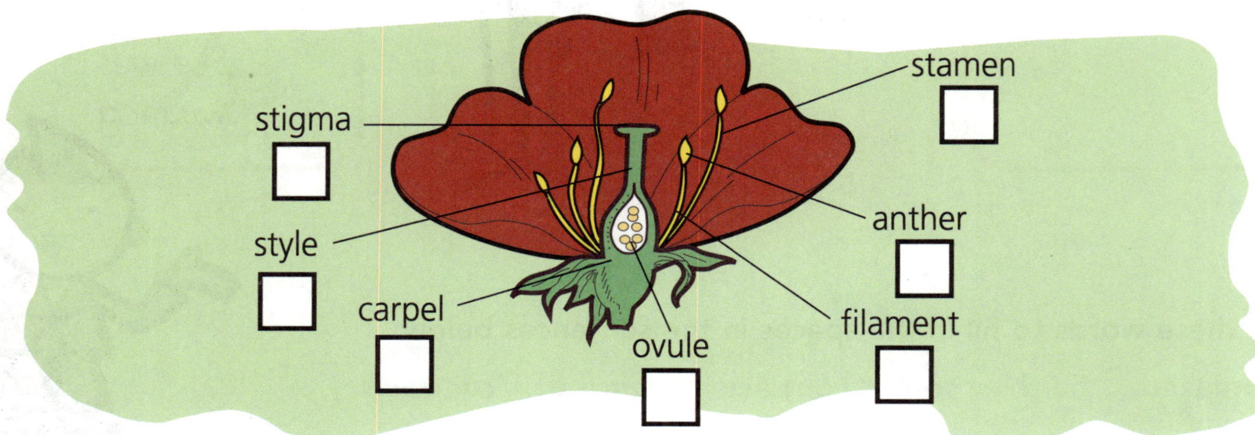

8 These three batches of cress seeds below were sown on the same day.

a Which batch do you think was left dry? ☐

b How did you choose? ____

____

____

c Which batch do you think was placed in a dark cupboard? ☐

d How did you choose? ____

____

____

9 Use the key below to identify these leaves.

Is the leaf made from several smaller 'leaves'?

- yes → Is the leaf shaped like a hand?
  - yes → horse chestnut
  - no → elder
- no → Does the leaf have a wavy edge?
  - yes → oak
  - no → beech

Leaf **a** is a ______________________ leaf.

Leaf **b** is a ______________________ leaf.

Leaf **c** is a ______________________ leaf.

Leaf **d** is a ______________________ leaf.

10 Look at this food chain.

owl ______________________
↑
shrew ______________________
↑
beetle ______________________
↑
leaves ______________________

Use one of the words **producer**, **herbivore** or **carnivore** to label each level of the food chain.

11 Heema has baked a meat pie. Once it has cooled, she decides where to store it. Think about what you know about micro-organisms.

A good place to store the pie would be ______________________________

because ______________________________

____

12 Use these words to complete the sentences below. Only use each word once.

elastic **transparent** **waterproof**

a Nylon is used to cover umbrellas because it is ____________________ .

b Glass is used to make windows because it is ____________________ .

c Elastane is used to make sports clothes because it is ____________________ .

13 Some children collected some information about three rocks:

	colour	hardness	other notes
rock A	white	could be scratched with a fingernail	rock made lines on other surfaces
rock B	grey	could be scratched with a knife	rock was thin and flat
rock C	grey	very hard – could not be scratched	rock had some glittery specks

The three rocks were slate, granite and chalk.

Which was which rock?

Rock A was ____________________ .

Rock B was ____________________ .

Rock C was ____________________ .

14 Choose one of these words to finish each of the sentences below to explain what is happening:

condensing freezing evaporating melting

a Washing dries on a sunny day.

Water is ________________________ .

b A bathroom mirror is covered in tiny drops of water.

Water is ________________________ .

c Tiny crystals of ice appear in a puddle on a cold day.

Water is ________________________ .

b An icicle drips in the sunshine.

Solid water (ice) is ________________________ .

15 You are making lunch. Is each of these changes reversible or irreversible?

	reversible	irreversible
a You put some soup in a pan and warm it up.		
b You make some toast.		
c You forget to drink your tea and it goes cold.		

16 Jack has a mixture of salt, tiny bits of gravel, and sand.

How might he get the salt out of this mixture?

Write down your ideas.

(Hint: You need to use sieving, then dissolving, then filtering and then evaporating.)

____

____

____

____

____

____

17 Some children make some circuits. None of the bulbs light up.
Say what is wrong with each circuit.

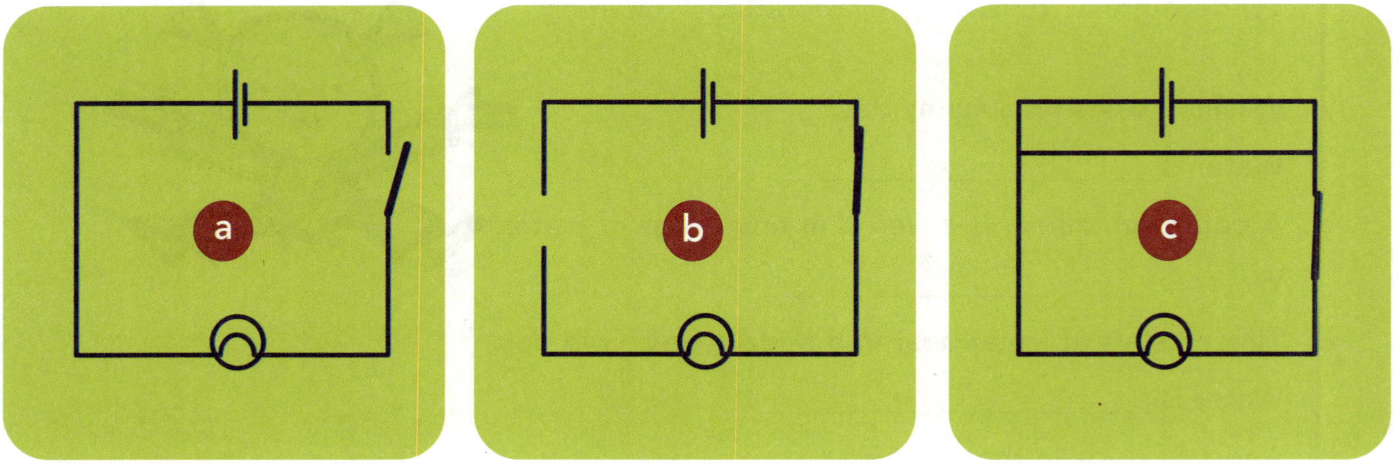

Circuit a: ______________________________

Circuit b: ______________________________

Circuit c: ______________________________

18 Look at these drawings where things are moving.
Name the forces shown by the arrows in each one.

Force a is ______________________ Force c is ______________________

Force b is ______________________ Force d is ______________________

19 You are investigating the effects of friction.

You decide to run a model car down a ramp and measure how far it goes. You change the surface on the ramp and see if it changes the distance that the model car travels.

Which of these things would you keep the same to make this a fair test?

- **a** The height of the slope ☐
- **b** The weight of the model car ☐
- **c** The wheels on the model car ☐
- **d** Everything except the surface of the ramp. ☐

20 In an experiment to test the strength of magnets, you use sheets of paper between the magnets and a paper clip.

Explain how you would measure the strength of different magnets in this experiment.

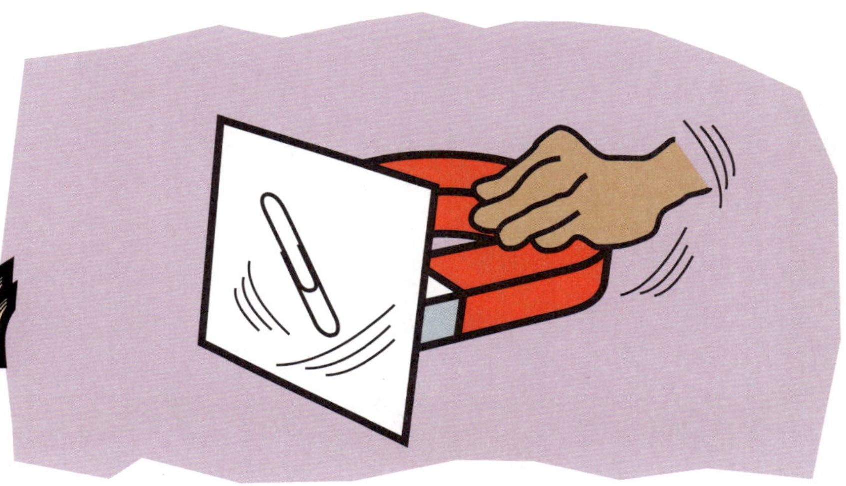

____

____

____

____

____

21 Draw a diagram to show what happens to the light from the torch when it hits the mirror.

22 Fill in the missing words.

- **a** Sounds are made when things v _ _ _ _ _ _ .
- **b** The loudness of a sound is called the v _ _ _ _ _ .
- **c** Whether a note is high or low is called the p _ _ _ _ .

Beyond the book

In the home

- **Looking at materials** – look at the way in which different materials are used around the home.

  How many different examples of absorbent materials can your child find?

  What materials have been used for building? Encourage your child to think about why different materials have been chosen. Make a list of all the natural materials used in your home.

- **In the kitchen** – encourage your child to look at the way in which different substances change when they are heated or cooled. Make scrambled eggs together to watch changes happen. Other good examples are making jelly, baking a cake and making ice lollies.

- **Medicine safety** – talk about the safe storage of medicines and why this is important. Help your child to make a warning label for your medicine storage.

Out and about

- **Looking at minibeasts** – take your child on a minibeast safari. Look for small creatures in unexpected places – under logs, in crevices in walls and on leaves. Talk about the need to avoid disturbing small animals, and encourage your child to look at the surroundings (habitats) in which they find them.

- **Looking at soil** – find a suitable place to dig a small hole. Encourage your child to look at the different layers seen in the soil. Look for plant roots, evidence of minibeasts and pieces of gravel or sand.

  Help your child to collect about half a cup full of soil. Place it in an old plastic drinks bottle and mix with water. Look at the layers as the soil settles. Remember you should always wear protective gloves when handling soil.

- **Shadows** – enjoy playing shadow games on a sunny day. Challenge your child to make long, tall, wide and thin shadows. Make a simple sundial together by placing a stick in the ground then watching and recording the positions of its shadow during the day.

In the shops

• **Solids, liquids and gases** – encourage your child to spot examples of solids, liquids and gases as you shop together. Point out some puzzling examples, such as ketchup (liquid), salt and sugar (solids), ice cream (solid) and fizzy drinks (gas and liquid).

• **Food chains** – talk about the different foods you eat, classifying them into those from animals and plants. Ask your child to think about the food chains involved. Encourage the use of terms such as producer (plants) and consumer (animals). For example, in a meal of egg and chips, the egg came from a chicken which was a consumer, eating grain, and the potato came from the potato plant which was a producer, making its own food, Encourage your child to think about whether humans are herbivores, carnivores or something of each (omnivores). Talk about the need for a balanced diet and dietary choices such as vegetarianism.

• **Trolley dash** – talk about the forces needed to move your supermarket trolley. Is it easier to push when it is full or empty? What sort of force is needed to make it stop or change direction. Look for places throughout the store where forces are in action: the conveyer, warning notices about slippery floors and using ramps.

Rainy days

• **Rain watching** – watch for condensation on cold surfaces such as the inside of single-glazed windows. Explain how this forms from tiny drops of water in the air (water vapour) meeting a cold surface. Make a rain gauge by placing a tall, plastic bottle in the garden. Mark the outside of the bottle in centimetres and measure how much rain falls each day. Don't forget to empty the bottle after each reading! Keep a chart of your findings.

• **Things to make:**

  • a poster about healthy living

  • a set of material dominoes (stick tiny scraps of different materials on the ends of oblong cards)

  • a book about the life cycle of an animal

  • a model tree, using clay or plasticene – make your tree come to life by adding tiny birds and animals

  • a set of shadow puppets using a lamp to cast shadows on a wall – make up a play and add sound effects.

Answers

Revise wise

Page 2
If you know your stuff reproduce
Try these
1 Living things respond to their surroundings.
2 true
Puzzle code N
On your toes Giraffes ride my new skateboard!

Page 3
If you know your stuff singer
Try these
1 life cycle
2 false
Puzzle code O
On your toes reproduction

Page 4
If you know your stuff plaque
Try these
1 plaque
2 false
Puzzle code W
On your toes Sugar left in the mouth, which is eaten by bacteria.

Page 5
If you know your stuff diet
Try these
1 true
2 diet
Puzzle code T
On your toes Fibre keeps the intestines healthy.

Page 6
If you know your stuff blood
Try these
1 clean the blood and make urine
2 true
Puzzle code H
On your toes organs

Page 7
If you know your stuff blood
Try these
1 false
2 heart
Puzzle code A
On your toes the ribs

Page 8
If you know your stuff water
Try these
1 wrist and neck
2 false
Puzzle code T
On your toes oxygen

Page 9
If you know your stuff brain
Try these
1 false
2 backbone
Puzzle code A
On your toes muscles

Page 10
If you know your stuff lengthen
Try these
1 get shorter
2 true
Puzzle code L
On your toes two

Page 11
If you know your stuff wine
Try these
1 medicines
2 true
Puzzle code L
On your toes the lungs

Page 12
If you know your stuff chlorophyll
Try these
1 photosynthesis
2 oxygen
Puzzle code T
On your toes carbon dioxide

Page 13
If you know your stuff sugar
Try these
1 hairs
2 true
Puzzle code H
On your toes water and nutrients

Page 14
If you know your stuff stamen
Try these
1 true
2 reproduction
Puzzle code E
On your toes To attract insects.

Page 15
If you know your stuff rain
Try these
1 pollination
2 false
Puzzle code W
On your toes stigma

Page 16
If you know your stuff anther
Try these
1 fertilisation
2 true
Puzzle code O
On your toes pollination, fertilisation, seed formation

Page 17
If you know your stuff pea seed
Try these
1 exploding pod
2 wind
Puzzle code R
On your toes spreading about

Page 18
If you know your stuff cabbage
Try these
1 The seed coat splits.
2 Food is stored in the seed.
Puzzle code K
On your toes germination

Page 19

If you know your stuff python

Try these

1 amphibian

2 fish

Puzzle code I

On your toes mammal

Page 20

If you know your stuff describe

Try these

1 bee

2 crane fly

3 spider

4 butterfly

5 centipede

Puzzle code S

On your toes A woodlouse has only 6 legs.

Page 21

If you know your stuff adaptation

Try these

1 for digging

2 to keep it warm

Puzzle code D

On your toes Two from: wings, good hearing, sharp teeth, claws.

Page 22

If you know your stuff horse

Try these

1 lettuce

2 grass

Puzzle code O

On your toes Beetle and caterpillar are herbivores; shrew, thrush and cat are carnivores.

Page 23

If you know your stuff camel

Try these

1 recycle

2 pollution

Puzzle code N

On your toes The number of field mice would decrease.

Page 24

If you know your stuff jellyfish

Try this

2 baby getting a cough

3 bread going mouldy

Puzzle code E

On your toes yeast

Page 25

If you know your stuff nylon

Try this

1 plastic

4 polystyrene

Puzzle code Y

On your toes Any from: it dries, hardens, gets lighter in colour and weight.

Page 26

If you know your stuff wood

Try these

1 transparent

2 strong

Puzzle code O

On your toes bendy

Page 27

If you know your stuff aluminium

Try these

1 conductor

2 insulator

Puzzle code U

On your toes Wood is an insulator so will not get hot and burn your hand.

Page 28

If you know your stuff impermeable

Try these

1 impermeable

2 cool

Puzzle code S

On your toes

Because it is very soft.

Page 29

If you know your stuff paper

Try these

1 false

2 false

Puzzle code E

On your toes clay

Page 30

If you know your stuff ice lolly

Try these

2 pastry

4 glass

Puzzle code E

On your toes solid

Page 31

If you know your stuff condensing

Try these

1 melting

2 condensing

Puzzle code H

On your toes

They will melt in the warm sunshine.

Page 32

If you know your stuff burning – it is a permanent change

Try these

1 reversible

2 permanent

Puzzle code O

On your toes reversible

Page 33

If you know your stuff sand

Try these

1 dissolves

2 solution

Puzzle code W

On your toes The pink powder has dissolved.

Page 34
If you know your stuff shredder
Try these
1 sieving
2 evaporating
Puzzle code S
On your toes a sieve

Page 35
If you know your stuff radio
Try these
1 on the metal part
2 series
Puzzle code C
On your toes It gets dimmer.

Page 36
If you know your stuff buzzer
Try these
1 true
2 using straight lines
Puzzle code I
On your toes False. They damage cells.

Page 37
If you know your stuff change colour
Try these
1 false
2 gravity
Puzzle code E
On your toes push, pull

Page 38
If you know your stuff energy
Try these
1 unbalanced
2 balanced
Puzzle code N
On your toes upthrust

Page 39
If you know your stuff a push away from the Earth
Try these
1 false
2 stronger
Puzzle code C
On your toes centre

Page 40
If you know your stuff streamlining
Try these
1 movement
2 true
Puzzle code E
On your toes friction

Page 41
If you know your stuff a small force
Try these
1 small arrow
2 Same direction as sharpener moves.
Puzzle code I
On your toes false

Page 42
If you know your stuff wooden spoon
Try these
1 true
2 those with iron in them
Puzzle code S
On your toes poles

Page 43
If you know your stuff blindfold
Try these
1 false
2 true
Puzzle code G
On your toes larger

Page 44
If you know your stuff shadow
Try these
1 false
2 false
Puzzle code O
On your toes predictable

Page 45
If you know your stuff child
Try these
1 true
2 false
Puzzle code O
On your toes light

Page 46
If you know your stuff pitch
Try these
1 false
2 volume
Puzzle code D
On your toes large vibrations

Page 47
If you know your stuff space
Try these
1 false
2 false
Puzzle code F
On your toes solids, liquids and gases

Page 48
If you know your stuff 1 month
Try these
1 28 days
2 gravity
Puzzle code U
On your toes roughly spherical

Page 49
If you know your stuff the sun moves during the day (False)
Try these
1 false
2 The sun is low in the sky in the East.
Puzzle code N
On your toes 24

Test questions

1 nutrition

2 **a** after breakfast
b so food doesn't stay on her teeth

3 **a** messages
b pumps
c clean

4 Her breathing was faster.
Her pulse was faster.
She felt hot.

5 **a** contracts, hard, relaxed
b relaxed, soft, contracts

6 **a** no
b plants need sunlight to carry photosynthesis.

7 M: anther and filament, stamen
F: carpel, style, stigma, ovule

8 **a** batch Z
b They have not germinated.
c batch Y
d They have grown long to try to reach some light.

9 **a** horse chestnut
b oak
c beech
d elder

10 owl – carnivore
shrew – carnivore
beetle – herbivore
leaves – producer

11 In the fridge because micro-organisms do not grow well in cold places.

12 **a** waterproof
b transparent
c elastic

13 A chalk
B slate
C granite

14 **a** evaporating
b condensing
c freezing
d melting

15 **a** reversible
b irreversible
c reversible

16 He sieves the gravel out of the mixture.
He adds water to the salt and sand and dissolves the salt.
He filters the mixture to remove the sand.
He evaporates the water, leaving the salt.

17 **a** Switch is in the 'off' position.
b There is a gap in the circuit.
c There is a short circuit.

18 **a** air resistance
b gravity
c upthrust
d gravity

19 **d** Everything except the surface of the ramp.

20 You could see how many sheets of paper each magnet will hold the paperclips through.

21

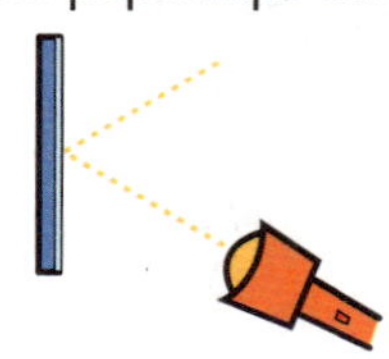

22 **a** vibrate
b volume
c pitch

Puzzle code

As you use this book, work out the correct answer to the puzzle code questions on each page.
Write the corresponding letter in the right spaces below, to figure out the coded message.

2 3 4   5 6 7 8   9 10 11

12 13 14   15 16 17 18   19 20   21 22 23 24

25 26 27   28 29 30   31 32 33

34 35 36 37 38 39 40   41 42

43 44 45 46   47 48 49 !

Mental Arithmetic 6

Teacher's notes and Answers

Name:..

Mental Arithmetic 6

compiled by E Spavin

0 7217 2449 3

First printed 1998

MENTAL ARITHMETIC is a series of seven books.

Introductory Book	0 7217 2446 9
Book 1	0 7217 2240 7
Book 2	0 7217 2241 5
Book 3	0 7217 2242 3
Book 4	0 7217 2243 1
Book 5	0 7217 2244 x
Book 6	0 7217 2448 5

Design and typesetting by
The Mouse House
Harrogate

Printed in England by
Dennis Print, Scarborough

INTRODUCTION

The content of this book builds upon and extends the work covered in the earlier books in the Mental Arithmetic series. It follows a pattern of 36 three-part Weekly Tests and 3 Revision Tests which could be used at the end of each term. Although the term 'Mental Arithmetic' implies that answers only are required, most students will need to use scrap paper and pencil, if only to jot down information taken from the various tables and graphs, and this should not be discouraged.

CONTENTS

The following is a short synopsis of the contents indicating the topics which are practised in each section and their coverage. The layout of the tests has been modified slightly from earlier books in this series in that the Part A Tests and the Part B Tests follow the same topic order from section to section. The Part C Tests now take the form of longer questions based on a problem-solving approach, allowing the topics introduced in Parts A and B to be developed in more depth. Each Section of twelve test papers is followed by a Revision Test.

Part A NUMBER, COMPUTATION, ALGEBRA

1 Four rules with positive and negative integers
2 Four rules with positive and negative integers (including remainders and brackets)
3 Numbers in words and figures; index notation, standard notation
4 Fractions, decimals, percentages, ratios, mixed numbers
Equivalence and ordering (including negative numbers and symbols <, >)
5 Calculations involving fractions, decimals, percentages and ratios
6 Four rules with decimals
7 Four rules with decimals (including remainders and brackets)
8 Approximations – to given number of significant figures – to given number of decimal places
9 Approximation of results of calculations; estimations
10 Algebra – substitutions
11 Algebra – solutions of simple equations
12 Squares, square roots, cubes, factors, multiples, primes, series

Part B MONEY, MEASURES, SPACE AND SHAPE, APPROXIMATIONS

1,2 MONEY
Four rules, shopping, costing, sharing, ratio
Percentages, profit/loss; buying and selling price; interest
Deposits and instalments; sales and discounts; foreign exchange

3, 4, 5, 6 MEASURES
Metric units, Imperial units, Conversions
Time
Compound measures

7, 8, 9 SPACE AND SHAPE
Circumference, perimeter, area, volume of simple 2D/3D shapes
Angle properties of simple 2D shapes including circles;
Pythagoras' theorem
Symmetry and order

Part C LONGER QUESTIONS

Coordinates	– identification and location – reflections, translations and mappings
Handling data	– graphs and tables, including the use of computer spreadsheets
Scale drawings	– using maps and charts
Probability	– calculating and using probabilities in simple situations
Number puzzles	– revision of number properties and use of mathematical symbols
Practical situations	– use of measures including length, area and money

REVISION TESTS

Each of the three Revision Tests consists of 25 questions similar to those in Parts A and B, and 15 further questions based on a problem situation as in Part C.